How to Start and Run a Home Day-Care Business

How to Start and Run a Home Day-Care Business

Carolyn Argyle
Illustrations by Beth Lemcke

A Citadel Press Book
Published by Carol Publishing Group

To all of the children that I have had the opportunity to provide care for in my home, to my own three beautiful children, and to my wonderful husband, Jim, without whose help and support my dream of writing this book would not be realized.

A Citadel Press Book
Published by Carol Publishing Group
Citadel Press is a registered trademark of Carol Communications, Inc.

Editorial, sales and distribution, rights and permissions inquiries should be addressed to Carol Publishing Group, 120 Enterprise Avenue, Secaucus, N.J. 07094

In Canada: Canadian Manda Group, One Atlantic Avenue, Suite 105, Toronto, Ontario M6K 3E7

Carol Publishing Group books may be purchased in bulk at special discounts for sales promotion, fund-raising, or educational purposes. Special editions can be created to specifications. For details, contact Special Sales Department, 120 Enterprise Avenue, Secaucus, N.J. 07094.

Manufactured in the United States of America

10 9 8 7 6 5 4 3 2 1

Library of Congress Cataloging-in-Publication Data

Argyle, Carolyn.
   How to start and run a home day-care business / Carolyn Argyle.
      p.   cm.
   ISBN 0-8065-1852-9 (pb)
      1. Family day care—United States—Handbooks, manuals, etc.
   I. Title.
   HQ778.63.A74   1997
   362.71'2'0973—dc21   96-29585
                                                              CIP

Contents

Foreword

So, you want to start a home day-care business. First you need to determine whether day care is for you. Are you well suited and qualified for the rigors of this business? Just as with any profession, this profession is not for everyone. Here are some things you might want to consider before deciding to make at-home child care your vocation.

Do you love children and do you enjoy spending time with children other than your own? Do you have plenty of patience and energy? Have you had experience baby-sitting or taking care of your own children? Do you have a home or apartment suitable for the care of children? Will you be able to communicate with parents about unpaid bills or other problems? Are you able to keep records, do paperwork, and think of ways to make your business more financially successful? Do you have enough toys and furniture or can you obtain what you need? Do you enjoy coming up with amusing and interesting activities for children of different ages? If you answered yes to these questions, you may be a candidate for opening your own home day-care business.

Now, don't be too hard on yourself. Maybe you've already given home day care a try without much success. Many home day-care providers quit during their first year because of problems they've encountered. Most home day-care providers have to learn from experience because they receive little training before getting into this business. An associate of mine decided to discontinue her day care. She said, "I think I just wasn't cut out for it." My reaction was, "Who is?"

Maybe there are some naturals out there. But many of us learn from experience, practice, training, and education. We can talk with other day-care providers or read books on the subject to learn how to be more effective and successful. I recall an experience in college which helped me to understand that, although initially something may seem awkward and difficult, one can become "good at it" through learning and the development of the appropriate skills.

I was a junior in college, majoring in Elementary Education, when I had my first part-time student-teaching experience. My professor was sitting in the back of the room evaluating my presentation. I stood up in front of thirty wiggly first-graders. I began teaching them about zoo animals. When in my presentation I got to the baboon, a child in the back of the room started making baboon noises. Then a whole chorus of baboon sounds ensued as other children followed this student's lead. Soon I felt like I was in the zoo. The class was out of control, in total chaos, and I didn't know what to do to stop it! When that horrifying experience was over and it was time to confer with my professor, he advised me to change my major. Well! I was a junior in college and was not about to start over with another major. I was bound and determined to be an effective teacher!

My second student-teaching experience went okay. I guess I had toughened up a little and I did an average job. I was happy to be average!

Then came my full-time "take-over-the-class" student-teaching experience. This time the professor observed my teaching of a third-grade class on four separate occasions. For each evaluation I received an "A". As I looked down at one of my evaluations, I glowed as I saw what had been written in large letters across the bottom of the sheet, "Great classroom control."

If you fail at first but have the desire to succeed, don't bail out prematurely! With practice and learning you can be successful. Maybe you are cut out for day care, but just a little rough around the edges. The fact that you're reading this book shows that you have the desire to run your own day-care business effectively. Are we all perfect parents to begin with? Surely not. Go ahead—give it another try! There's something to be said for the old adage, "If at first you don't succeed, try, try, again!"

What are the advantages of having a home day-care business? I believe the number one advantage is that it allows you to be home with your own children while earning needed extra income. It also allows you to spend more time with your husband or significant other, as your outside-the-home employment situation or your own child care needs may require you and your husband to work different hours. A recent television program illustrated how some working mothers of a dual-income household actually have less disposable income as a result of the second job. In some cases, financially, the family would actually be better off if the mother stayed at home due to the additional expense associated with the second job (e.g., taxes, clothing or uniforms, commute, child care, cost of eating out more). The researchers interviewed recommended doing some kind of work in the home like child care. Many child-care providers, with their own young children, find that it is more profitable to manage a home day care than to be employed outside the home. As a home day-care provider you eliminate child-care expense, commute expense, uniform expense, and can generally deduct enough expenses to limit your tax liability.

Some mothers go to work to receive the health-care benefits or are divorced or single and need to have a career outside the home. Some mothers like to get out and prefer that to staying at home. However, if you are a mother who prefers to be home with her children, yet wants to earn extra or needed income, a home day-care business may be for you. Also, there are some grandmothers who find home day care very rewarding.

My motivation for starting a home child-care business began when I needed to earn extra money temporarily to pay off some of our debts. Although I had a college degree in Elementary Education, I didn't want to start a teaching career away from home while my children were small. I wanted to be with them. After pursuing some less-than-satisfying outside-the-home employment opportunities, I began a home day-care venture.

As I began the endeavor, I found that I enjoyed being an entrepreneur. I experienced a sense of pride in running my own business. I enjoyed planning the activities that I would do with the children and setting my own rules. I enjoyed being with my own children and they enjoyed helping me prepare for the lessons and parties. My son always had friends to play with and really enjoyed having the children come. He was able to have a quality preschool education at home. My son learned about getting along with other children, sharing, following, leading, and being a good citizen.

I hope this book will help anyone interested in starting their own home day-care business or anyone who works with children. This book will address the topics of licensing, insurance, advertising, day-care policies, keeping your home and belongings from destruction, keeping children healthy, getting your payments, providing quality preschool education, organizing and cleaning your home, feeding the children, establishing rules and disciplining children, bookkeeping and taxes, and more.

Today, the need for quality child care is a growing concern. A recently released national study published by the Children's Defense Fund found that "child care at most centers in the United States is poor to mediocre, with almost half of the infants and toddlers in rooms having less than minimal quality." It was found that only one in seven received a rating of good quality overall, and even fewer (only 8 percent) were found providing good quality care for infants and toddlers. When children are cared for in these minimal-quality conditions, it affects their health, safety, emotional well-being, and intellectual growth. Good child care providers are in demand.

Good parents are seeking quality child care for their children. They will not settle for poor or mediocre care if they can help it. A couple came to me looking for child care for their three-year-old son. They had been through four day-care homes in the past year, all of which were unsatisfactory to them. It was very frustrating for them and difficult for their child. After being with me for a while, they finally felt like they could relax and not worry. Not only did they feel that he was in an environment where he was safe—but also happy and thriving. That is the goal we need to shoot for—quality care where children thrive!

For this reason, I hope to pass on some of the things that I have learned from my experiences. I have made my fair share of mistakes and keep learning from them. Note that the suggestions in this book are just that, and if you find alternatives that work better for you, that's great too. The important thing is that we are professionals and that as professionals we are constantly learning and trying to improve ourselves. Researchers have concluded that the first three years of life represent the most rapid period of human development and the experiences during these years can have profound effects on the child. The job of a day-care provider is very important when you think of the lives of these children that you, as a day-care provider, are helping to influence. While in our care we can do our best to give them love, take care of their physical needs, and provide a quality educational environment. We can be a good influence on them by doing our best to help meet their emotional, physical, moral, and intellectual needs while they are in our care.

No part of this book is intended to conflict with existing child-care laws or licensing regulations. The reader is responsible for compliance with laws and regulations governing child care and family child-care licensing, as well as for ensuring the safety of the children in his or her care.

Permission has been granted by the National Center for Missing and Exploited Children to excerpt information from their guidebook *Child Protection: Guidebook for Child-Care Providers*.

1

Preparing for Business

Naming Your Business

The first thing you need to do, even before getting your license, is to identify a name for your business. You may wish to use your own name (e.g., Carolyn's Child Care or Denise's Day Care). You may like to pick a descriptive or fun name such as: Teach and Care, Love a Lot, or The Happy Clown Day Care. You may use the name of your business on your day-care license and in your advertisements.

Licensing

Whether or not you get a license will be up to you. However, state laws will dictate the number of children you can legally care for without a license. Such restrictions will vary from state to state. One state, for instance, may require you to be licensed if you care for more than the children from one family, whereas another state may allow you to care for up to four children without a license. Some states place restrictions on the number of children in your care under the age of one or two. You will need to identify the applicable laws in your state. To obtain the telephone number of the licensing bureau in your area, you can call the Children's Defense Fund at (202) 628-8787 (ask for Child Care Division) or direct an inquiry to your local Child Care Resource and Referral Service.

State licensing requirements may include a home safety inspection (covered electrical outlets, locked away knives/dangerous chemicals, accessible fire extinguisher/first aid kit, etc.), fingerprinting, and tuberculosis test. In addition, some states may require CPR training and more extensive background checks including information on the day-care provider's spouse and backup provider. The trend is toward making day-care homes safer, thus requirements will, in all likelihood, be on the rise.

Even though state certification is not required for caring for four children in Arizona, I opted to become certified in order to receive the following benefits: referral of clients on government-subsidized programs, the ability to obtain day-care liability insurance through my homeowner's policy, and the increased capability of generating new business (i.e., parents tend to be more attracted to a home day-care center that is under the state's watchful eye). A more detailed listing of benefits is provided at the end of this section.

Many cities offer a state orientation session which provides information on how to get your license. You can also receive written information about the requirements through the appropriate state agency. Given that you will be in a position to ask questions and solicit more information, I recommend that you attend an orientation session and then follow the instructions provided in applying for your license. After meeting the requirements (such as inspections, form completion, background check), you may have to wait a few weeks or even a few months to receive your license.

Once you are licensed, you may receive announced or unannounced visits from time to time by the state's licensing authorities. If you are obeying the rules of your state, you don't need to worry about these visits. An example of a licensing report for an unannounced visit is on page 133. You should carefully read all of the rules with which you agree to comply when you are licensed or certified. For example, corporal punishment was prohibited in thirty-nine states as of 1993 when these data were collected. This means no physical punishment is acceptable, such as spanking, hitting, slapping, striking, pinching, shaking, and the like. You may be required to sign a statement that you agree to use only acceptable forms of discipline as listed on the form you sign. In talking with a new client, I was informed that I could spank her children. According to the law in most states, you should not spank a child under your care, even if the parent or guardian gives you permission.

There are other rules that you may need to agree to, such as: having an open-door policy, identifying a backup provider, maintaining a nonsmoking environment, having fire drills, and so forth. Again, these rules vary greatly from state to state. As of 1993 when the following statistics were gathered by *Parenting* magazine and then verified and updated by the Children's Defense Fund: 25 states required liability insurance, 42 required parental access, 19 states banned smoking, 35 states required both smoke detectors and fire drills, 17 states required some CPR, 27 required some first aid training, and 45 states required basic immunizations. These were requirements for licensed family day-care homes (requirements vary for child-care centers).

If you wish to care for more than five or six children, you may need to apply for a special license for a group day-care home and be required to hire an assistant. Here is an example of requirements for a group day-care home (Arizona):

- submission of an application fee every three years
- an actual residence environment with certain square footage requirements
- an accessible fenced play area
- a fire inspection
- general liability insurance coverage
- fingerprinting and FBI review of all personnel and adult household members
- CPR certification
- child first aid certification

- regular inspections by the Department of Economic Security for compliance with basic health and safety requirements
- an open-door policy to parents
- one caregiver to five children must be maintained at all times

Along with the requirements with which you must comply come the benefits of being "certified by the state." Some of these benefits may include (Arizona):

- eligibility to contract with the government to provide subsidized services to referred clients
- the opportunity to lawfully serve the number of children that are in your care
- free orientation and ongoing training
- free technical assistance from the Office of Child Care Licensure
- free newsletter subscription
- inclusion on a public listing distributed by the Office of Child Care Licensure
- access to listings with other information and referral programs
- an increased awareness of basic health, safety, and developmental needs of children

State certification is a symbol of professional commitment that may add value to your child care services.

Insurance

Day-care insurance is available and can be added to most homeowner policies. You may wish to look into the rates. You may find that it is not too expensive and is well worth it. The current rate for home day-care insurance may range from $80 to $400 per year depending on the coverage you want and the number of children in your care. Some insurance companies can add a rider to your home insurance policy to include day-care liability insurance. This is perhaps the least expensive way to pay for day-care insurance. Some organizations make available liability insurance for their members as a group insurance program. The group buying aims to provide better coverage for a better price for its members. A sampling of day-care insurance programs is listed on page 129. Having day-care insurance may save you from the worry of a lawsuit for which you are not prepared. A friend of mine provided day care for a boy who, while in her care, was injured. His parents were threatening to file a lawsuit. She became very concerned about losing everything she had. Based on her experience, she highly recommended day-care insurance coverage.

Accidents may occur while children are in your care even though you childproof your home, make it as safe as possible, and watch the children well. One day my son bit another child on the back while playing alligator. I didn't see this happen. The parent of the child called to ask whether someone had struck her child with a belt. She described marks that she had found on her child's skin. I was taken aback. I tried to reassure the mother that no one had struck her child with a belt. The next day I observed my son playing alligator again and biting this child on the back. When I explained to the parent what happened and how I had spoke to my son regarding the matter, she was relieved. I was grateful for this parent's understanding and trust in me as a day-care provider. However, I also recognized that not all parents would have been so understanding. Some may not have accepted the explanation and may have pursued the matter further. From that perspective, the incident reaffirmed for me the need for liability insurance coverage.

A recent newspaper article entitled "Crisis in Child Care" by Victoria Harker and Judy Nichols appeared in the *Arizona Republic* (April 7, 1996, pp. A1 *ff.*). The article points out that although most of the state's day-care centers are safe, others are deadly. Some children have drowned, been beaten, neglected, and abused while in day care. It is no wonder that parents are alert to any indication of mistreatment.

It is important to read your day-care insurance policy carefully, because the coverage may not be as extensive or as comprehensive as you think it needs to be. When looking into day-care insurance, ask whether the policy covers the following: bodily injury to day-care children in your home, or while on field trips; bodily injury to members of the public, or damage to property; lawsuits arising out of providing, or failing to provide proper professional services; injury to children or sickness alleged to have been caused by meals served in your home; injury to children, or sickness alleged to have been caused by someone else's products used by you; expense of medical bills arising out of accidents to children even though the injury was not your fault; and defense in court for civil suits alleging sexual abuse by you or your helpers. Also, determine the liability limits of the coverage.

If you do not wish to purchase day-care insurance, the alternative is to maintain an affidavit regarding liability insurance and keep this signed statement on file which states that your facility does not carry liability insurance (refer to page 137). This does not, however, affect the right of parents to bring legal action against your facility.

Start-up Equipment and Toys Needed

Before you open your doors to day care, you will need some equipment and toys. Here are some items that infants and toddlers may need:

- blocks
- clean bedding (separate bedding for each child, laundered at least weekly)
- cribs or Portacribs (preferably a separate crib or Portacrib for each child)
- high chairs
- infant outdoor swing
- infant seat
- playpen
- riding toys (kiddy car, scooter, etc.)
- rocking horse
- rubber or plastic balls
- small slide

- spare diapers and wipes
- spare pacifiers and bottles
- stuffed animals and dolls
- swing
- walker
- washable changing pads

Toys to be used by one- and two-year-old children should be durable, clean, nontoxic, too large to swallow, and have no sharp edges. Toys should be inspected regularly to ensure that they are not hazardous.

Preschoolers and school-age children may need some of the following:

- art supplies (crayons, markers, Play-Doh, paint, scissors, paper, etc.)
- bed, cot, or floor mat
- blocks, Legos, Lincoln Logs, Tinkertoys
- books
- children's furniture (small table and chairs, small fold-out couch, etc.)
- doctor kit
- dolls
- dress-up clothes
- each child's own clean sheet or blanket (laundered weekly)
- educational computer programs (if computer is available)
- educational toys (alphabet, numbers, shapes, colors)
- games
- musical instruments
- play money
- play telephones, cash registers, and play dishes
- puzzles
- riding toys
- sandbox
- small figurines (popular characters, toy soldiers, dinosaurs, farm animals, etc.)
- swing set
- work papers (math, reading, phonics, etc.)

Other start-up equipment (some of these items are necessary and some are just nice to have):

- childproof cabinet locks
- childproof stove knob covers
- cordless telephone
- covered diaper pail
- egg timer
- fire extinguisher
- first aid kit for car
- first aid kit for house
- flannelboard
- outlet covers
- smoke detectors
- stool in the bathroom next to sink so children can reach to wash hands
- television set
- VCR

In chapter 3, I have added some helpful ideas for organizing your toys and day-care supplies for easy accessibility and practical arrangement.

Advertising

In most cases, in order to get customers you must advertise. Don't get discouraged if it takes a few months to build your client base.

Five common ways to advertise your day-care business are:

1. *Child Care Resource and Referral, other referral agencies, and government contracts.* Contact your local office of the Child Care Resource and Referral agency to become listed with them. The agency may send you a form to complete or have you respond to questions over the phone. Parents who use the referral service may contact you directly or the agency may notify you of a client it has referred to you first. The parents receive a list of the day-care providers in their area (refer to page 132). I received about 50 percent of my business through this agency and there was no cost associated with

the service. Also, the government contracts with day-care providers for child care for low-income families. Typically, the contractual requirements may include: fingerprinting of all adults in the household, limited number of children, liability insurance, annual visits, thorough on-site inspections, CPR and first aid training, a backup provider, and completion of required forms. Other organizations also provide referral services (e.g., employer-affiliated groups that assist employees in obtaining child care).

2. *A sign in your front yard or on your house.* This is how I received about 25 percent of my business. A sign may sound simple enough, but it can really attract those who are looking for a local (close by) day-care provider. You can post the sign at all times or only put it up when you need to attract new business. The cost of the sign is minimal. Some wood, stencils, paint, and a little talent can make for a very attractive sign. However, you may want to think twice about adding your phone number to the sign. Those wanting to burglarize or vandalize your house may call the number to see if you are home.

3. *Word of mouth.* This is how I received 25 percent of my business. A working mother employed in my husband's office requested my services as a result of their conversations about day care. Also, friends or acquaintances of my clients made inquiries as a result of communications received about my service. A known commodity is always easier to sell than an unknown.

4. *Flyers on bulletin boards or distributed in some other way.* In order for a flyer to catch someone's eye, it must be colorful and appealing. You may wish to have your phone number printed and perforated several times along the bottom so that the prospective client can tear off the number. The easier you make it for the customer, the more likely it is that he or she will place that initial call.

5. *Newspaper advertising.* This form of advertising may be effective in attracting new business, but placing an ad can be costly. Often, in a mid- to large-size city people will call who don't

live or work in your immediate vicinity and therefore are not interested. You may receive calls from people with unusual child care needs for which you do not provide (for example, weekend or night care). In addition, many are not comfortable with finding a home day-care provider through this medium. However, if you have a unique service or live in a small community, newspaper advertisements may work for you.

What Do Parents Look For?

In soliciting new business or maintaining your existing clientele, it is important for you to know what parents look for when selecting a child care provider. In a recent survey, parents ranked the factors that influenced their decisions in selecting a child care facility. The number one factor identified was the training and experience of the provider. Therefore, any relevant training and education you can obtain will be beneficial, such as early childhood development, CPR, training workshops. Other factors with high ratings include: the number of children in your care, inside appearance of the home or center, phone manner of the provider, and cost. You will want to keep these factors in mind as you continue to develop your business.

I discovered in talking with my clients why they had discontinued taking their children to previous day-care providers. Among their complaints were that the provider transported the children in the car too much, the provider's home was messy and unsanitary, the provider didn't pay enough attention to the children, the provider didn't adequately meet the child's needs (food, diaper changes, medication), the provider complained about the children, and/or the child learned bad language or other bad habits in day care.

I asked the State of Arizona's Child Care Resource and Referral office what their customers have requested in regards to child care. The following information is based on customer responses for approximately a twelve-month period beginning July 1, 1995 through June 18, 1996. Approximately 14,000 customers contacted CCR&R for child care for approximately 20,000 children.

- 58 percent of families requested referrals to child-care centers
- 88 percent of families requested referrals to family child-care homes
- 3 percent of families requested referrals to in-home child care
- 2 percent of children needed a child-care provider who had training or experience working with children with special needs
- 13 percent of children needed child care which provided transportation
- 81 percent of children needed full-time child care
- 18 percent of children needed child care during the evening hours
- 1 percent of children needed overnight child care
- 13 percent of children needed child care after school
- 8 percent of children needed child care before school
- 16 percent of children needed child care during the weekend
- 2 percent of children needed child care which offered a preschool program
- 28 percent of children needed child care which was contract or certified by the Department of Economic Security

Of the customers who completed follow-up surveys, 73 percent reported having difficulty in searching for child care. The three most frequently cited problems during a search for child care are:

- cost of child care (16 percent)
- quality of child care (16 percent)
- location of child care (11 percent)

Answering Phone Calls

When potential clients call looking for a day care provider, answer questions openly and honestly. Offer any information you believe is pertinent, (such as your qualifications, program, fees). Ask them questions. You need to learn as much about them as they would like to learn about you. Invite them to come and talk to you and introduce their child/children to you.

Policies and Forms

When you meet with the parent(s), provide them with the forms they will need to complete and return to you, including a Provider-Parent Agreement-Contract and a Day-Care Policies sheet (refer to pages 134 and 135). It is important for the client to understand your policies and acknowledge his or her agreement by signing the appropriate form. In addition to providing the parents with a copy, you will want to keep a signed copy for your records. These policies will help protect you from being taken advantage of in various ways (for example, receipt of late payments or having a child picked up late). Each policy should clearly state the consequence(s) of not complying with what has been agreed to, such as charges for late payment. Take time in drafting your Day-Care Policies sheet. Try to anticipate the various scenarios which could play out to the detriment of your business. Some possible areas to cover in your policies sheet include: sick policy, hours your facility is open, the charge(s) for child care, late fees, form of payment accepted, who provides the food, diapers, etc., and who may pick up the child. You may add to your policies sheet later if you come across a new problem or situation. Once again, the client must be given the opportunity to read and agree to the new stipulation.

The other forms that you will have the client complete are required and provided by your state licensing bureau. If you are not licensed, I recommend that you develop similar forms. The forms to be kept in the file prepared for each child include: Provider-Parent Agreement-Contract, Day-Care Policies sheet, Identification and Emergency Information, Affidavit Regarding Liability Insurance, Notification of Parent's Rights, Transportation Permission (refer to pages 134, 135, 136, 137, 139, and 145), and Food Program Enrollment Form. Add the name of the new child along with the parents' names, home and work phone numbers, address, and the child's birthday to your day-care roster. Post the roster in a highly visible area of your facility, such as the refrigerator. An example of a day-care roster is provided on page 141.

What to Charge

What to charge will depend upon the going rates for child care in your area. You may want to review your local Resource and Referral listing in getting an idea of what others are charging within your locale. I have found that setting my fees somewhere near the middle of the market-determined range has allowed me to attract and keep clients.

You may choose to have a straight hourly rate or a daily or weekly rate. This is up to you and what you think parents would prefer. Charging by the hour may be viewed as more equitable since some parents leave their children for longer periods of time (longer days). However, most parents would prefer to pay a set daily rate rather than an hourly rate. For the parent, a set daily rate is more straightforward and is easier to anticipate and budget for. In addition, parents tend to believe that they will experience greater cost savings and flexibility with a daily rate. I charged a set daily rate for eight- to nine-hour days and a slightly higher daily rate for ten- to eleven-hour days. This is up to you.

In addition, you may offer a discount to parents with two or more children in your care. Whether or not you offer discounts depends on what the common practice is or how competitive the business is within your area.

Will you charge when the children do not come? Some day-care centers and homes only charge for days the children are in attendance, while others charge a straight weekly fee regardless of attendance. Other practices include not charging for vacations planned in advance and charging a partial fee when the child is not in attendance. To a large extent, the market may determine your practice. If you do proceed with a set rate regardless of attendance, you may want to convey to the parents how you can maintain a low caregiver/child ratio by charging in this fashion. If charges are attendance based, then you must increase the caregiver/child ratio to cover the lost income which results from children not being in attendance. A low caregiver/child ratio allows the day-care provider to provide more one-on-one attention. In addition, you may want to remind the parents that they receive paid vacation and sick leave in connection with their employment, so it is reasonable for the day-care provider to be compensated when their child is sick or absent.

Forms of Payment

Some parents receive governmental assistance for their child care. If you accept these children in your care and have the choice, choose to receive the voucher payments directly from the governmental agency rather than from the parent. Under such an arrangement, you don't have to be concerned about receiving payment. However, in terms of frequency, your payment may be limited to a monthly check and you can experience "in the mail" delays.

Parents should be encouraged to pay promptly and as agreed upon (for instance, at the beginning of each week or the end of each week). It is always upsetting not to get paid on time. Inform the client through your Day-Care Policies sheet of the consequences for paying late. Also, have consequences for bad checks, for example: first bad check, $10 charge; second bad check, all payments must be made in cash, money order, or cashiers check.

Late Pickup

Parents who pick their children up after closing time or the agreed-upon time do not always realize what an inconvenience they are creating for the day-care provider. A late pickup can significantly cut into your family time and perhaps the dinner hour. Inform the client, at the time of the occurrence as well as in your introduction of day-care rules and policies, that late pickups will result in an additional charge (such as $1 per minute) or you will have to ask them to have a friend or relative pick up the child. Not only is it frustrating for you to have the parents late, but if the late pickups continue, the child may feel somewhat abandoned by his or her parents.

Charging for Part-timers

Your part-time rate should be higher than your full-time hourly rate to compensate for the additional coordination required in caring for part-timers. When I began my day care and only had one child of my own, I accepted both part- and full-timers in my care. Although they did not all attend at the same time, I ended up with a dozen children enrolled in my day care (some for morning preschool, some after school, etc.). It required significant coordination in making sure that I didn't go over my limit of caring for no more than six children at one time. In addition, getting part-timers integrated into current activities, retrieving coats and toys, and talking with parents added to the confusion and strain.

Later, I dropped the part-timers and only accepted full-timers. In retrospect, I could have raised my part-time rate by 50 cents an hour, which would have allowed me to significantly reduce the number enrolled without adding full-timers.

If you are making a third the amount of money per day or per week for a part-timer than you would make with a full-timer, it probably is not enough. Making a third the amount of money would translate into needing three part-timers for the amount that could be made with one full-timer. If you are making half or more the amount for a full-timer, then you probably are charging enough for your part-timers. Currently, I have one part-timer who pays $6 per day for three hours and the full-timers pay $12 per day for eight to ten hours. I am making half the money for the part-timer and providing care for about a third the hours of the full-timers.

Charging for Infants

Many day-care providers charge more for infants. Infants do require more one-on-one attention and special care. They cannot feed themselves and they cannot participate in group or structured activities. For this reason you may wish to charge a little more for infants. However, this does not mean that infants are always more difficult to tend. Many infants sleep for a number of hours. In general, infants require a different kind of care than toddlers and older children.

Charging for Transportation

You must decide whether or not you will provide transportation for parents who need children picked up or taken some place (e.g., school, baseball practice, bus stop). Think of a fair price to charge for this service to help cover not only gas, but vehicle wear and tear. Most employers will reimburse employees at the rate of about 30 cents a mile for the use of the employee's car for business-related travel. Such a rate of reimbursement could be applied to your day-care transportation as well. In transporting children you must have a seat belt available for each child and adequate auto insurance coverage. Most states require children under a certain age to be placed in special child safety seats.

Payment Receipts

You should provide the parents with a receipt upon payment of services. Be sure to keep a carbon copy of the receipt for your own records. Some parents will also ask you to provide your social security number on the receipts for tax purposes.

2

Rules and Discipline: Dealing With a Variety of Personalities

Rules

When you initially meet with a client, you provide him or her with an outline of your day-care policies and solicit agreement by having him or her sign the form. You then continue to enforce the provisions of this contract. When you begin caring for a child, you should proceed in the same fashion. Start by reviewing your rules of behavior and conduct with the child. Ask the child if he or she understands and will follow and obey these rules. Treat the child with the same respect that you extend to the parents. Then consistently enforce the rules. Orienting a new child represents an opportunity to review the rules with all the children in your care.

You can tailor the rules of your facility to your needs. Rules should be introduced and presented to the child as a collection. When needed, you can remind the children of certain individual rules. Each rule should also stipulate a consequence for breaking the rule.

An example of a set of rules is provided:

Rules

1. No hitting, kicking, disturbing, or causing harm to other children.
2. Listen during circle (or preschool) time and allow others the same privilege.
3. No bad language, name-calling, or other such unacceptable behavior.
4. Respect other people's property and the property of the day-care home.
5. Obey all instructions of the day-care provider.

Consequences

1. The child will be reminded that the behavior is unacceptable according to day-care rules.
2. The child will go to the time-out corner or table (TIME-OUT).
3. If the child continues to break a rule; the day-care provider will speak to the child's parents.

Remember that physical punishment is *never* acceptable. If you are unable to curtail inappropriate behavior effectively, it is wise to involve the parents and let them work with the child at home in helping to teach the child acceptable behavior. It could be that the parents are unknowingly reinforcing or modeling the unacceptable behavior at home and are willing to work with you in addressing the situation.

Some Responses to Unacceptable Behavior

1. *Time-out.* When children disobey one of the day-care rules or become disruptive or out of control, they may need to be removed from the situation for a few minutes. The rule of thumb is one minute per year of a child's age. Thus, a three-year-old child may be placed in time-out for three minutes. Select a particular chair or quiet corner as the time-out place. Use this method only occasionally when it's truly needed. Overuse of this method will decrease its effective-

ness. Also, apply this approach in a consistent manner with all of the children. Don't single out one child and constantly put that child in "time-out." Find other ways to help that child improve his or her behavior.

2. *Change unacceptable behavior to acceptable behavior.* When children are running through the house, organize a game of tag outdoors or play a record and let the children dance. If a child writes on the walls, give the child crayons and let the child draw constructively. If a child says a bad word, provide the child with an alternate word to use.

3. *Explain to the child the consequences of his or her actions.* This helps the child to understand why he or she should refrain from such behavior. Try to speak in terms of the child's own interests as well as yours. For instance, "Please don't pound on the TV. The TV costs a lot of money to replace. If it is broken, we won't be able to buy a new one until we have saved up enough money. This means that we won't be able to watch TV for a while."

4. *Allow the child to make amends.* If a child breaks something, let him or her help fix it. If a child throws toys around, have him or her pick them up.

Time to Trade

One of the most common problems and cause of conflict in young children is the inability of children to share toys and other things. The concept of sharing is hard for small children to understand. They want everything to be MINE. To deal with this, I employ a method I refer to as "Time to Trade." The approach has helped playtime run much smoother with less conflict. It has also helped teach the concept of sharing. Every five minutes I call out "Time to Trade" and the children must swap toys with each other. This way, if a child wants to play with a toy another child has, he or she knows that he can play with it when I call out "Time to Trade." As a result, the child is not always asking me if he or she can play with that toy now and he or she is not grabbing it away from the other child. This works well during bicycle time when children have to share bicycles and some children must take turns sitting out. It also works well with children playing with different kinds of balls or books, or with the swings on the swing set. The child feels secure that for five minutes that toy is his or hers and no one can take it away.

"Time to Trade" can also be used when problems arise. For example: One day you are outdoors with the children. Two children are playing in the sandbox. One child tries to grab a shovel away from the other child. Say to him or her, "He was playing with that first. In five minutes it will be 'Time to Trade.'" In five minutes, when you call out "Time to Trade," the two children trade their toys. The children get accustomed to "Time to Trade" and it is amazing how quickly the children obey when "Time to Trade" is called out. It works!

Positive Reinforcement

Rewards

You can give rewards as incentives for positive behavior. You may wish to reward children for accomplishing tasks, helping clean up, sitting quietly, or participating in a lesson or activity. You can be creative in rewarding children. Of course, rewards aren't necessary for everything and should not be overused. However, a spoonful of sugar helps the medicine go down. Ideas for rewarding children include:

- award ribbons
- buttons
- candy machine
- certificates
- prize bucket
- stickers.

Candy Machine   I have a candy machine that I fill with peanut M&Ms, or a mixture of M&Ms, peanuts, and raisins (I try to keep it fairly healthy). When rewarding children, I give them a penny and let them get their treat. They enjoy doing this.

Prize Bucket I use an empty ice cream bucket decorated and labeled Prize Bucket. When I want to reward the children, I let them pick a prize out of the bucket (toy party favors, stickers, pencils, suckers, Fruit Roll-Ups, granola bars). I use the prize bucket to reward children who have completed enough tasks to fill up a row on their Fun Work for Prizes Chart (refer to chapter 4).

Positive Verbal Reinforcement

Praise children who are behaving well! This transfers the attention from the misbehaving children (who are trying to get attention by misbehaving) to the well-behaving children. The misbehaving children will see that if they behave they will receive attention. For example, if you say, "Wow, Johnny is sitting very still," the wiggly children are more inclined to start sitting still. Praising the children who are behaving is sending the same message as scolding those who are misbehaving without reinforcing the inappropriate behavior.

Praise children often throughout the day. Make comments such as, "I'm proud of Rachel for how well she is learning to use scissors," and "I'm really proud of you, Thomas, for learning how to swing by yourself now." When you only acknowledge the misbehaving children, you are (most of the time without realizing it) ignoring the children who are behaving well.

Role Modeling

How often do we see parents out in public who have had it "up to here" with their toddler or preschooler? Oh yes, if you're a parent then you should know what "up to here" means. We've all been there. It's what comes next that is up to us. All too often we see this picture: a parent screaming at their child, slapping or spanking them in hopes of forcing or frightening them into behaving better. Or do they do it to release their own frustration? The result—a child crying and screaming—total chaos! What is your reaction when you see this? Do you feel sorry for the parent because the parent has a child who requires such measures? Or are you appalled at the parent for behaving in such a way? My reaction tends to be more aligned with the latter.

Self-control and patience are traits a parent and a child-care provider must develop and possess. Teaching by example is perhaps the most effective way of modifying behavior. Therefore, the parent who hits and yells at his or her child is sending what kind of message? Not to hit and not to yell? Actions speak louder than words. Don't be a hypocrite by saying one thing and doing another!

Believe it or not, you set the tone for your day-care home. If you exhibit kindness, consideration, politeness, warmth, love, and are upbeat and positive, the children will follow your example and this is the type of atmosphere you will have in your day-care home.

Maintain Realistic Expectations of Behavior

To have realistic expectations of children's behavior, we need to be familiar with concepts of child development. Observing children can also further our understanding of child development. We should take note of how teachers and other day-care providers effectively interact with children at different levels of development. You will need to use a variety of approaches based upon the age and ability of the children. For example, you may have a thirty-minute lesson prepared for preschool. During this time you can expect the three- to five-year-olds to sit still and listen to the lesson. However, you may need to allow the younger children to play with toys or get involved in some other activity when they are no longer able to focus on the lesson. Do not punish a child for not being able to do an activity that is not in line with his or her age and capability.

When a child is behaving in a way that may be harmful to him/ herself, others, or someone's property, you may need to redirect the child's behavior to a more positive and constructive activity. Such an approach is much more effective than disciplining a child who is not old enough to understand the consequences of his or her actions. For example, a thirteen-month-old child pulls the hair of another child. Rather than punishing the child, quickly respond by indicating that pulling hair is a "no-no," remove the child from the situation, and redirect the child's attention elsewhere.

Another example of maintaining realistic expectations of behavior is a parent sitting in a waiting room with two children ages two and four. After the first hour, the children become restless and noisy. The parent becomes frustrated and angry. Many parents react by threatening, yelling, and/or spanking their children. However, this is not fair to the children, who are doing as well as can be expected under the circumstances. Alternative reactions to the situation may include: taking the children for a walk, giving the children something to play with, or reading them a story.

The following poem, which I wrote, helps to illustrate where a two-year-old may be at in his or her development:

Terrible Twos

Rules are for breaking—that's what he thinks.
This kind of behavior really stinks
For when I'm not looking, I'm afraid
All kinds of disasters and messes are made.

But when I am looking an angel he is
Sweet as a cupcake
Calm as a mouse
We really enjoy having him in the house.

But when I'm not looking, I do fear
I can smell disaster near.
He glues my stockings to the wall
He breaks my window with his ball.

He eats the icing off the cake
He hides my keys for goodness sake!
He writes all over important papers
Oh, you wouldn't believe all of this kid's kapers!

He wears my jewelry and my shoes
Yes—you've guessed, he's in his terrible twos!
He eats a bite out of every cookie
And then he says, "Hey, Mommy, looky!"

He cuts his hair— he throws his food
He really gets in a crazy mood
When I'm not looking
Or I'm in cooking.

But we'll forget it—yes we lose
Because he's in his terrible twos.

Dealing With Personalities and Behaviors

In interacting with my day-care children, I have experienced many different personalities. And it is with a sense of joy and fascination that I observe children. They want to learn and explors sand they have an innocence and love for everyone that is refreshing. The positive traits of each child are easy to deal with (cuteness, sweetness, kindness, etc.) and you will see these personality traits in all of the children under your care. However, how do you deal with the difficult side of each child? The following are some common personality traits and behaviors, and approaches/techniques for effectively responding to them.

Whining

Many children whine on occasion, but some children whine constantly. For the most part, children whine to get your attention. Children value the attention of adults and they need it. Often, children in day care don't get enough attention because their parents are busy working long hours, and when not at work, are taking care of household duties and pursuing outside interests. Some children only have one parent and it is hard for one working parent to give the child all of the attention he or she needs. As a day-care provider, it is a challenge for you to give each child enough individual attention. Attempt to spend a few minutes chatting with each child one on one. Also, consider the following in response to whining:

1. Establish a rule that the children may get what they are asking for if they ask politely, but they will not receive it if they whine.
2. Respond to the child's request when he or she asks in an appropriate manner.
3. Instead of just saying "Stop whining!" provide the child with an alternative, such as "Ask politely."
4. Teach the children the tone of voice that you prefer—but also demonstrate what they sound like to you. Explain that when they sound like that you will not be able to grant their request, but when they use the appropriate tone of voice you will acknowledge them.

Temper Tantrums or Pouting

Temper tantrums most often occur when a child is emotionally overwhelmed or just extremely tired. However, some children have temper tantrums regularly because they have learned that this is a way of getting what they want. My philosophy for responding to temper tantrums is to "ignore it and it will go away." If the answer is "no" to a child, the answer should remain "no" even if the child throws him or herself on the floor and kicks and screams. You need to remain calm under such circumstances and not let the tantrum get to you. Don't give the child attention for such behavior. You will find that if you do this, the frequency of the tantrums will decrease.

I have often observed parents giving in to temper tantrums. I hear them say things like, "He threw a fit so I let him go with them," or, "She kept pouting so I let her have her dessert first." Giving in to temper tantrums is a great way of reinforcing the behavior.

If you have a child in your day-care center who often throws tantrums or pouts when he or she doesn't get his or her way, you may also need to solicit help from the parents. You can ask them to help you with your efforts in curtailing this type of behavior by not reinforcing such behavior at home.

Some children only have temper tantrums on rare occasions

when they are emotionally overwhelmed or extremely tired. If so, a nap or rest may be the answer to the problem, and you will find the child in good spirits after he or she sleeps.

Crying and Being Victimized

Some children seem to cry all of the time. This is not necessary. Of course, it's appropriate for children to cry from time to time. Crying represents a normal way of expressing and releasing emotion as a reaction to a difficult or painful situation. But for some children, I'd say that 90 percent of their crying is unnecessary. When the crying appears to be unnecessary, avoid being too sympathetic. Under such circumstances, a "You're okay" would be a more effective response than "Oh, you poor baby." Also, attempt to point out to the child more constructive ways of dealing with the situation (for example, tell the child to avoid the other child for a while; or, ask the child to say what he or she needs at that moment). It is good to give children hugs (or some show of affection) often throughout the day, but not to reinforce unnecessary, constant crying.

Crying, in infants who cannot speak, is another issue. Infants must cry to communicate. Respond quickly to their needs whether it be a bottle, diaper change, burping, a nap, and so on.

Some children let themselves become victims. These children are crying a lot because of little things that other children do to them. They let everything bother them. They know that they can get your sympathy if one of the big kids teases them. Unfortunately, the victim's reaction to the bully tends to reinforce and feed into the behavior of the bully. The bully teases in order to get a reaction. It may take some time, but you must, whenever possible, help the victim differentiate between the "biggies" and the "nonbiggies." The "biggies" are issues which the child should learn to address himself or herself either through avoidance, communication, problem solving, or some other way than crying. You should always express a willingness to help and support the child in responding to these types of issues (for example, child not included in an activity, child hit or kicked, child's toys are taken from him or her). The "nonbiggies" are issues which the child should learn to ignore and to which you will tend not to respond, such as name calling, making faces, unintentional accidents by other children.

Bullying

Some children seem to enjoy teasing or picking on other children, especially children smaller than themselves. When these children play with other children someone ends up getting hurt or crying, but not the bully. Oftentimes, the child doesn't seem to understand that even though he or she may enjoy teasing other children, they do not enjoy it. It's necessary to remind the child that if he or she doesn't like others picking on him or her, then he or she should refrain from picking on others. The child needs to realize the importance of controlling his or her own actions. Provide the child with specific examples of behaviors you find inappropriate. Time-out may be necessary whenever such behaviors are observed. Taking away the privilege of playing with the other children for a little while may also be needed. Try to help the child put himself or herself in the other child's shoes, so to speak. Share with the child how the other children feel when they are teased.

Lying

Most children will lie from time to time. They have not yet learned the importance of telling the truth. You must teach them the importance of telling the truth. Some child development experts believe that children who lie are actually exhibiting a sign of intellectual growth. To be an effective liar the child exhibits the ability to quickly think and make up stories, control their emotions, and take the listener's point of view. Lying is a skill children learn. It is used for avoiding punishment. Some ways to respond to lying are:

- Let the child know that you take lying seriously. Help him or her understand the negative consequences of lying.
- Help the child understand that the lie, in some instances, can

be as much if not more of an issue than whatever the child is lying about.

- Keep in mind that some lying by young children is normal. If the child lies excessively, it could be a bad habit derived from fear of the consequences of the truth or fear of certain people.
- Help the child understand that when he or she lies, the child usually is found out at some point in the future. Also, people will be less inclined to believe the child in the future if he or she is not honest.

My oldest son, Matthew, has always been a bright child. He is good at math, and at the age of three could quickly put together 200-piece puzzles intended for six- to fourteen-year-olds. I may always remember an incident in his life when he concocted an intricate lie. I call it the "Bean in the Nose Incident" and look back on it with humor, although it could have been serious at the time. He was in first grade. I picked him up from school and he had a tissue covering up a bloody nose. Walking home and talking with him, I found out that he had a bean up his nose. I guess his teacher didn't know this. (In his classroom, his teacher used pinto beans for math addition and subtraction lessons.) I asked him how it got there. He said that at lunch recess he was playing hide-and-seek with a group of children. When he had his eyes closed to count, a kid stuck a bean up his nose. He didn't know which child did it. He said that he had told the lady on recess duty. So, first I was concerned about the bean because it was so far up his nose I couldn't see it and it could have been a serious problem. I had him blow his nose, and fortunately the bean came out. Then, we went back to the school to talk to his teacher.

I told his teacher what my son said had happened. She asked me if I considered the possibility that Matthew had placed the bean in his nose during math time. She told me that if I wished to write down Matthew's story and send it with him to school the next day, she would look into it. I couldn't imagine my son making up the whole story, so I wrote down what my son had described and the teacher proceeded in investigating the matter. The next day, after speaking with the playground attendant, the teacher informed me that the attendant had indicated that Matthew had not talked to her about this. When I mentioned it to Matthew, the truth came out. Matthew had actually put the bean in his own nose.

I was embarrassed. I didn't think my son would tell me a lie like that and stick with the story until he was found out. I made Matthew aware of the consequences of his lie (another child could have been falsely accused, the time and effort expended in conducting the investigation, our mutual embarrassment). Matthew, also learned, and I reinforced, the fact that eventually the truth did come out, that is, he didn't avoid anything by lying). Matthew also learned that I was as concerned about the lie as I had been over the bean in his nose.

Biting

Biting is a normal part of a child's early development. Biting most often occurs between the ages of one and a half to three years. When a child is upset with another child, one way he or she may respond is by biting the other child. When this happens, respond quickly and let the child know that biting is not appropriate under any circumstances. Help the child identify other ways to respond, such as to move away from someone bothering him or her, or to ask for help. Small babies may bite because they have the need to teethe on something. You may wish to provide them with a teething ring or toy.

In my day care, at one time, I had 3 two-year-old boys. They were going through the biting stage and my son, who was four years old, decided to copy their behavior even though he was too old for that. So, we had the "Alligator Incident." The boys were all playing alligator outside and biting each other on the back. My son, however, being four years old, really had a hard bite. He didn't realize the harm that was resulting from his behavior. After speaking with the children about the seriousness of biting, the biting problem ended.

Bad Language

You don't want to have bad language in your day-care home and you don't want your own children picking up on it. If it is a problem, you may need to talk with the child's parents. For children old enough to understand, you can explain to them that a particular word is not used in your home. Give them an alternative word or phrase that they may use. I have found that the children old enough to understand this will respect you and use appropriate language in your home.

Shyness

Some children have a tendency to be shy. However, you can help them become more participative with you and the other children. Let the child gradually become comfortable with new situations. Don't refer to the child as being shy. Children tend to live up to the perceptions of those around them in exhibiting behaviors which are consistent with the label. You wouldn't want to go around referring to a child as "fat," "dumb," or "ugly," and the same goes with "shy." A child will, out of habit, use shyness as an excuse for getting out of doing things he or she doesn't want to do. But, by the same token, shyness may prevent the child from doing what he or she really wants to do.

I had a five-year-old girl in my care who initially was so shy that she just stood in the corner and wouldn't come join in. I didn't make a big deal out of it but just continued with my normal routine, allowing her to observe me. As her comfort level with her new environment increased, I gradually introduced her to new activities and got her involved with the other children. Later you wouldn't know that she was the same quiet girl who had stood in the corner. She was an exuberant, happy child and a welcome addition to my day-care home.

Tattling

More likely than not you will have a few tattletales in your day care. Is tattling good or bad? What can you do about it?

To begin with, I wouldn't label tattling as either good or bad. Sometimes I think it is necessary in order for me to be aware of what's going on. However, it can also be unnecessary when it takes the form of petty or cruel gossip.

If my two-year-old gets a marking pen and is writing on the walls, I want my seven-year-old to tell me. If a three-year-old is putting a sharp object into an electrical outlet, I want another child to tell me. If a child is running around hitting children with a stick, I need to know.

Some things are important for you to know. Sometimes the tattler is just trying to bring justice to a world that can seem so unjust. Therefore, I recommend that you don't punish the tattler. You always want children to feel comfortable in coming forward with a concern. However, there are tattletales who enjoy and are constantly tattling on others over petty things. There may be a number of reasons why the child might exhibit this behavior. Perhaps the child feels that he can build himself up in your eyes (favored status) by pointing out the faults of other children. Perhaps the child is doing it to get more attention. Perhaps the child thinks he or she can avoid getting in trouble by getting other children on the proverbial "hot seat." Try to help the child overcome the tattling problem by understanding and dealing with the underlying cause (getting attention, getting back at other children, seeking approval). Help the child see the difference between needful tattling and unnecessary tattling. Be sure that the way you react to the tattling does not reinforce the unnecessary tattling.

I'm Telling

"I'm telling!" yelled Sarah Ann Browning.
"I'm telling on Tommy for always frowning.
I'm telling on Wendy for taking my seat.
And laughing and tickling and stepping on my feet."

"I'm telling!" screamed Sarah Ann Browning.
"I'm telling on Pete for always clowning.
I'm telling on Bobby for spilling his juice.
And Ben for whispering secrets to Bruce."

"I'm telling!" cried Sarah Ann Browning.
"I'm telling on Joe for merry-go-rounding.
I'm telling on Amy for taking my swing.
I'm telling on Russell for not saying a thing."

"I'm telling!" shouted Sarah Ann Browning.
"I'm telling on Katy for almost drowning.
I'm telling on Joe for kicking and splashing.
And diving and swimming and almost crashing."

"I'm telling!" roared Sarah Ann Browning.
"I'm telling on Bobby for pounding.
I'm telling on Richard for scattering my toys.
I'm telling on Daniel for making so much noise."

"I'm telling!" said Mother.
"I'm telling you, Sarah Ann Browning.
To stop tattling—get the clue!
No one is perfect and that includes you!
Until you are perfect I will have no more tattling.
I'm tired of the telling, yelling, and battling."

Sarah Ann Browning's face went red.
She ran and threw herself on her bed.
She cried and cried until she no longer could.
And then she returned and she understood.

"Momma, I'm telling!"
"I'm telling—it's true!
I'm telling—I'm sorry and that
I LOVE YOU!"

Strong-Willed, Disobedient, or Bossy

What happens when you discover that you have a strong-willed, disobedient, or bossy type in your day care? You probably will experience a power struggle at your very first encounter. This happened to me. I was exhausted after that day. What was I going to do? When I told this child to do something she'd say, "No, I don't want to." Well, the next day was not quite as bad. As this child began to recognize that I was in control of things at my day care, things got better. Be strong, firm, but kind. I like to look to Mary Poppins as my role model. She has fun with the children, loves them and is loved by them, but at the same time is very firm.

This does not mean that the attributes of being strong-willed or bossy are always negative. I have found that you can use these traits to your advantage and at the same time allow the child to have some freedom to be in control too. Allow the bossy child to be in charge by playing "teacher." Let the child be in front and show the flashcards to the other children and tell the children if they are right or wrong.

Provide the disobedient child with a choice instead of telling him or her what to do, when it is possible. For example, instead of "You need to lay down for a nap now," say "Would you like to sleep on the bed or the fold-out couch?" The latter is more likely to yield compliance than the former. Sometimes a child just may be tired of always being told what to do.

Use positive discipline. One day at my day care, a child dumped sand on a baby's head. I told her this was not nice and that she needed to sit in time-out for three minutes. She refused to go to time-out. I had perhaps two seconds to decide how to react to this. What should I do? Here were some of my options:

- Pick up the child angrily and put the child on the time-out chair.
- Spank the child and put the child on the time-out chair.
- Threaten the child with "I'll tell your mommy if you don't go to time-out."
- Give in and give up—she wins (or does she?) No! She learns only that she can get away with it the next time.
- Yell at the child to try to get her to go to time-out.

The above are all don'ts. These represent negative ways to discipline. Make disciplining a positive experience in which children are learning something positive—how to behave!

Think of positive ways to react to these types of situations. I decided to present the child with a choice rather than issuing a command. I said, "When you do something like this to hurt another child you need to go to time-out. That is our rule. Would you like to sit at the picnic table or the little table for three minutes?" She chose the little table and sat there for the designated amount of time.

Another option for dealing with a child who does not want to obey would be to help the child understand why he or she needs to obey you, rather than punishing him or her for not obeying. The way in which this can be done is to let the child see that you are not the only one giving commands. Throughout the day the children are often giving you commands, such as: "I want a drink of water," or "Tie my shoe." If a child does not wish to obey you, explain to him or her that you can't obey him or her if he or she won't obey you. You have a mutual relationship in which both of you are giving and receiving. The child understands how important it is for you to obey his or her commands and therefore quickly obeys yours.

The Problem Child

I decided to add this category after talking with a friend, also a day-care provider, and after thinking about some of my own experiences. She told me that she had two boys, ages six and ten, who were driving her crazy! In the short couple of months that she had watched them, they had broken a window, the roof of their shed, and kicked the front door in. They like to bother and annoy her own children, and even her husband doesn't like to come home from work until after they have gone.

Generally, the children that I have seen like this are sometimes older and have been through a lot, such as parents divorcing, poor day-care situations, only one parent, or the parent working long hours. Sometimes these children have physical or behavioral problems, such as asthma, hyperactivity, or learning disabilities.

The movie *Problem Child* is funny, but the reality is not. When my friend said that she would have to stop watching these children when summer came, the children said, "There goes number five." The parents of these children go through a number of day-care providers each year, not because the parent can't find one good enough, but because the day-care providers can't tolerate the children's behavior. What do you do if you get these children in your care?

First of all, we never label the children as "Problem Children." We should never place any negative labels on children. They may have poor self-esteem and will live up to any labels placed on them. You have the right to give them a try or to drop the children. It is better to drop the children from your day care than to keep them if the situation isn't working out. If you wish to give them a try, realize that these children, like all children, need lots of love and attention. They aren't getting enough of it at home and they aren't home long enough to get enough. So, first try to give them love even when they aren't lovable. Talk with them about areas that they need to improve on and praise them when they try to improve their behavior. Keep the children busy so that they don't have lots of idle time to get into mischief. Find out what they like to do. Become their friend.

3

Cleanliness, Organization, and Home Preservation

Home Preservation

As a day-care provider using your own home, one of your concerns will be how to keep your home and belongings from wearing out and being damaged. This was a particular concern for me when I first started my day care in our new home. I have found that if you take certain precautions, you can cut down on the amount of wear and tear.

Relative to use of their home, some day-care providers limit access to certain rooms. One child care provider I know has a beautiful new two-story home. She only uses the kitchen, dining room, a den, a bathroom, and the backyard as her day-care facility. This leaves the rest of her home untouched. Her children's own rooms and the living areas of the home are left undisturbed. She decorates the day-care part of her house with colorful posters and pictures of the alphabet and animals. It makes for a neat and clean atmosphere which impresses her clientele.

Some day-care providers turn their garages into child-care rooms. The children stay in the converted room when not outdoors, leaving the rest of the home untouched. Such an arrangement may be workable if your garage has adequate climate controls, windows, and is childproofed. However, some parents are not comfortable with their children being cared for in a garage.

Another day-care provider I know uses her basement for day care. A basement may be fine if it has an emergency exit, that is, direct access to outdoors. When I began doing day care, I used my entire home. Now, my preference is to keep two of the bedrooms and one bathroom entirely off limits. I mostly use a family room dedicated to day care use and the kitchen table for eating and art work.

No matter how much of your home you use for day care, be prepared to take precautions in preserving it. The following items require protection:

Carpet

If you are concerned about your carpet getting soiled or stained, you can purchase rugs with designs for children (dinosaurs, city streets, alphabet). I place rugs down in my day-care room during normal business hours to protect the carpet. Initially, I didn't do this and my carpet became soiled quickly. I incurred the expense of hiring carpet cleaners every few months. In addition, my carpet was permanently stained by spilled medication (liquid Tylenol) and vomit (a toddler who drank Kool-Aid before arriving at my day care).

Furniture

If you have nice furniture you don't want the children to use, you can purchase children's furniture for your day-care facility. If you don't have much money to spend, little plastic chairs can be purchased at dollar or discount stores at a reasonable cost (typically, $1). Also, little plastic tables are available. Children's furniture can be purchased at toy stores or through catalogs. In addition, you can purchase small couches or chairs that pull out into beds or you can purchase cots, mats, or toddler beds for nap time. The children in my day care enjoy the little couch that unfolds out into a bed.

Walls

Teach children not to mark on walls. Besides instructing them, keep all markers, pens, and crayons out of the reach of children. Only bring these items out for supervised activities. Use only washable markers. Walls can also be damaged by children throwing toys or other items. Make sure that children understand that throwing toys is unacceptable because they can damage property and hurt other children.

Windows

Invariably you will get little hand prints on windows, but they can be cleaned off. Real damage to windows and window coverings include: breaking a window, breaking a screen, damaging screen doors, and damaging blinds or curtains. Do not allow children to throw objects near or out of windows (e.g., balls, Frisbees), and do not allow them to play in curtains or touch blinds. A five-year-old boy in my care threw a Frisbee and broke my window. This was particularly discouraging because I had only been in business two months and the child had only been in my care one week. I had only made $25 for watching him part-time and the cost of replacing the window was $135. I was concerned about losing money in this line of work. Fortunately, the broken window represented the most significant damage experienced that year.

I have had to repair a window screen because a child threw a toy through it. The screen only cost $9 to repair. I learned to have the children play away from window screens. I have a window near the table where the children use scissors for art projects. One child decided to cut my horizontal blind. If you can, keep tables away from windows.

Toys

If you have some expensive breakable toys or toys with sentimental value, I recommend that you keep them out of the reach of your day-care children and not use them during your hours of operation. Have toys available to the children that are sturdy and durable or toys that you wouldn't miss too much if they were broken or damaged. You can pick up used toys at garage sales and thrift shops. Be sure to wash and disinfect each toy with bleach. If you have a swing set or large play apparatus, expect the equipment to get used and worn and be prepared to purchase new equipment when necessary. Be sure toys are age-appropriate. An older child may be too big for a swing set or tricycle.

Personal Belongings

Keep personal items out of the day-care room(s) or out of reach if possible. Files can be locked in a filing cabinet. Videos can be secured in a video cabinet. Books can be stored on high shelves.

Neatness and Cleanliness

According to a recent survey, cleanliness (or appearance) is one of the top five factors considered by parents in deciding upon a day-care home. What is the secret to keeping your home clean and neat while doing day care?

1. Have a place for everything and everything in its place. This may require some organization. Labeled baskets and plastic containers may help in organizing items. Believe it or not, once I got into organizing things, I began to think it was fun! It's stress relieving to have an organized house. I spend much less time looking for things.

    When you purchase anything new, such as toys, books, or videos, find a place for the item. Let's say, for example, you purchase some toy dishes. At the same time, purchase a twelve-quart plastic container (or the appropriate size container). Label the container and find a place on the shelf of the toy cupboard or closet for the item. See chapter eight for hints about the washing of toys.

2. Clean up after one activity before going on to the next. (Children can help clean up!)

3. Teach children not to reach for toys or other things unless they ask you first. Children should learn to put away whatever they get out. If the children have difficulty returning toys as directed, only permit them to get out one box of toys at a time. Don't allow the children to get out another box until they return the toys to the first.

4. Have an organized schedule of events for your day and, as a group, proceed with one event at a time.

5. Don't keep too many toys and books where children can easily get them. If they want a toy or book which is out of their reach you can get it for them. Any toys or books within the children's reach, they have been trained to put away.

6. Have children throw trash in the garbage. Teach them not to be litterbugs. If they have a Popsicle, tell them if they want another one (or the other half) they must first return their wrapper and Popsicle stick to you or place them in the trash receptacle.

7. Make cleaning fun. Have a clean-up song. After toy time have the children sing the clean-up song as they put all the toys away.

8. At the end of the day, reward all children who helped clean up with a prize from the prize bucket, or candy or peanuts from the candy machine.

9. Have the children only eat food in the kitchen, outdoors, or in specific areas where you allow food. Sweep and wipe up after meals and art projects. Send the children outside to play or to watch videos in the next room while you clean up.

10. Keeping the house clean and organized as you go is easier than trying to clean up after a lot of messes. Vacuum and tidy up right before the parents visit as part of your routine. Extra cleaning (bathrooms, windows, etc.) can be done during nap time, after closing time, and on weekends.

Organization

Toys

Don't place all of the toys in one toy box or container to be mixed together. Some toys are small and belong together as a set. Also, with all of the toys in one container, it makes it difficult for the child to find the toy (or toys) he or she wants. Instead, an economical and practical way of organizing some of your toys is to place them in shoe-box-size plastic rectangular containers with lids. Group toys in these containers by type (for example, cars, toy figurines). The containers are available at many discount stores for $1 to $2 a piece. Some of the brand names include Tucker Housewares, Sterilite, and Rubbermaid. I recommend the Tucker Houseware brand because the lid of the box has a tighter fit than some of the others. For about $20 you can have a nicely organized and fun toy area. The containers don't take up a lot of room because they are stackable. They can be stacked in a closet, on shelves, or in a toy cabinet. (At a local discount store, I found a cabinet with three shelves that will accommodate twenty-one containers.)

The containers are see-through so that children can view the contents. Place labels on both the front and back ends of the container to help you identify the contents. Secure labels with clear mailing tape. If desired, place decorative stickers on the ends of the containers to help children identify the contents (dinosaurs, cars, colored shapes, dishes, animals, Disney characters, doctor or a doctor kit, baby or baby toys, doll, and doll clothes). Children enjoy taking out one container, playing with the toys, and then returning it for another container. Small children cannot open the containers without assistance, which helps to minimize the scattering of toys. Toys that I keep in these containers include: kid meal toys, snap-together toys, play money, doctor's kit, baby toys (rattles, keys, etc.), card games, toy soldiers, toy dinosaurs, cookie cutters and rolling pin, Play-Doh, Play-Doh molds, shapes and colors, pegboard pieces, number puzzle and ABCs, peg numerals, colored stacking circles, toy people and animals, and Disney and other toy figurines (Lion King, Aladdin, Pocahontas, Ninja Turtles, and such).

The larger twelve-quart plastic containers (approximately $3 each) may be used for items such as games, Lincoln Logs, blocks, Legos, Barbie dolls, doll clothes, and play dishes. These containers should also be labeled and kept on a closet shelf.

The large under-the-bed size plastic containers are available, depending on size, for about $6 to $20 each. These are useful for storing dress-up items (hats, purses, capes, costumes, etc.), large construction paper, coloring books, and worksheets. In addition, large decorations for birthdays and other holidays can be kept in these type of containers. (Refer to page 147 for photos of organized toy areas).

If you have more money to spend, you can purchase cabinets and tote trays specially designed for day-care facilities through catalogs such as Environments (refer to page 127), or these items may be purchased from teaching supply stores. There are many attractive and functional storage units available.

Toy Box   I place large one-piece toys, such as trains, trucks, dolls, toy guitar, toy cash register in a toy box or chest. I let the children play with these toys during free play or toy time.

Shelves or Cupboards   Shelves (wall, closet, or cupboard) are an excellent location for covered stackable containers as well as some large toys. If you have stuffed animals, you may want to consider storing them in baskets on the shelves. In addition, a hammock designed for the purpose of storing/displaying stuffed animals can be hung in the corner of the room.

Preschool and Craft Items

Preschool and craft items can also be stored in shoe-box-size plastic containers. As with toys, use labels to identify the contents of the container. Contents may include: string and yarn; chalk and erasers; scissors, glue, tape, hole punch, and staplers; stamps and stencils; stickers; paint; crayons and markers; paintbrushes and sponges; Play-Doh molds; Play-Doh; fishing pole and fish; tickets; Popsicle sticks; fasteners, rulers, safety pins, straight pins, paper clips, tacks, buttons, pencil sharpeners, and pencils; alphabet flashcards; and birthday cards. Organized supplies are much more presentable than a stuffed drawer or closet and represent less time spent looking for what you need. When you have several energetic children to watch, you don't want to spend your time looking for a safety pin or the chalk and erasers.

Children's Personal Belongings

You need to have a place for each child's personal belongings. Children bring stuffed animals, blankets, diapers, wipes, medications, and the like to your home. You can use plastic baskets/ containers (stackable) or "cubbies" (divided cabinet or shelves). Label each basket or cubby with the child's name. I prefer stackable baskets (refer to page 148) in which the contents can be easily retrieved from the front of each basket. The baskets use little floor space and can easily be moved if necessary. Place craft items and notes to bring home in each child's basket or cubby. Coats may be placed on a designated coat rack or in a closet, and shoes can be located in a shoe box or rack specifically set up for the children. Parents should be able to pick up all items for their child easily at the end of the day.

Diapers

Diaper bags may be placed in a designated area, such as near the diaper pail or diaper changing area or on a readily accessible shelf. In organizing your supply of diapers, you may wish to use stackable baskets labeled with each child's name (refer to page 148). When the diaper supply runs low, ask the parents to bring you a full bag of diapers (you can tell them in person or leave them a note in their child's basket). Or you may request that the parents bring a daily supply of diapers in the child's diaper bag.

Books

I prefer to keep all books up high on a shelf and only get them down at storytime or when I choose to let the children look at books, such as naptime). This helps to maintain the condition of the books and prevents the children from cluttering up the room with them.

Videos

I keep videos in a video cabinet under lock and key. I only open the cabinet for movietime, when I allow the children to select a video. This helps prevent damage and cluttering of videos.

Music Tapes

Music tapes can also be damaged. I recommend that you keep the cassette tapes out of the reach of children.

VCR

Keep the VCR up high or, if that's not possible, use a childproof device specifically designed to prevent children from placing foreign objects into the VCR. My two-year-old placed a TV remote into our VCR, the unit hasn't worked well since the mishap.

Files

A filing cabinet is a must for storing and organizing day-care forms, preschool materials, and so forth. In my filing cabinet I keep the following:

Drawer #1
- advertising ideas
- attendance sheets
- bookkeeping system
- business expense receipts
- child-care news
- curriculum guides for preschool program
- food program—menu plans and forms
- tax forms (e.g., W-10s)
- state licensing forms for the parents to fill out
- file with information on each child
- medication authorization and record forms

- music song books for preschool program
- patterns
- flyers announcing activities to parents (Carnival, Santa's Secret Workshop, I Like Brown Day, Rodeo Day).

Drawer #2 In this drawer I store items from my preschool program. If you do not subscribe to a preschool program you may have your own materials to file such as:

- flannelboard stories and figures (e.g., Cinderella, Elves and the Shoemaker, Christopher Columbus, The Little Red Hen). Store your flannelboard stories in 9″ x 12″ manila envelopes with the title marked on the front.
- educational games (e.g., Alphabet Concentration, matching games)
- visuals for songs (e.g., "Five Little Speckled Frogs," "Wheels on the Bus")
- letters and numbers, which I keep in manila envelopes with the letter on the outside of each envelope for the children to see. Inside each envelope are pictures cut from magazines of things that start with the letter.
- language skills flannelboard pictures.
- paper dolls (which have been laminated or covered with contact paper)
- finger puppets.

As your supply of materials grows, you may need to purchase an additional filing cabinet.

Missing Piece Jar

What I call the "Missing Piece Jar" is probably the most important container I use aside from the prize bucket. For ease of access (you don't have to open the lid), you may prefer to use a basket. I put in this jar or basket all the miscellaneous items (Legos, blocks, toy soldiers, puzzle or game pieces) I find around the house that didn't get picked up when toys were put away. These items are often found under couch cushions, behind furniture, or lying on the floor. Before I started to use a missing piece jar, I would either stuff the items in an untidy drawer (never to be seen again) or throw them away (too lazy to return the item to its proper container). Over time, I would end up with unusable puzzles and games, or fewer and fewer Legos and blocks for the children to build with. I add items to the jar as I find them. However, I only return the pieces to their original locations at the end of each week or when I have the time. In the meantime, if a child is missing a game or puzzle piece, he or she knows to look in the missing piece jar. It works out very well.

Prize Bucket

I use a large ice cream bucket decorated with stickers as a prize bucket. In this container I have a number of small toys (like party favors), stickers, suckers, fruit snacks, granola bars, pencils, and so on. I use the prize bucket to reinforce appropriate behaviors as described in other sections of this book.

Games and Puzzles

Ideally, games and puzzles should be together on a designated shelf in the day-care or bedroom closet. Puzzle boxes often break apart and need to be taped together periodically. If necessary, use other containers such as plastic freezer bags, diaper wipe boxes, or plastic containers. Cut the picture from the original puzzle box and tape or glue it to the outside of the new container.

Through continual use, game boxes start to break apart. Rubber bands can be used to help keep the boxes together, or you may choose to keep them in twelve-quart rectangular plastic boxes. Be sure to keep the instructions and to label the boxes if necessary.

Other Items to Organize

You may wish to use a large laundry basket in organizing outdoor play equipment (for example, balls, mitts, bowling pins). You may also want a special container or box for swim equipment (extra towels, floaters, sun block).

4

Planning Your Day—Preschool Ideas and Activities

Routines

Children need to have some predictability in their days to add stability to their lives. A regular routine helps children be prepared for what's next and can help children eat and sleep better. For example, the children will become accustomed to nap time following story time. Most children will have reconciled themselves to the fact that they will need to sleep after a story is read to them. Having a routine helps you to be sure that you include all of the necessary activities in your work day, such as: meals, snacks, diaper changes, hand washing, learning activities, naps, fresh air, exercise, and fun. Having a regular routine does not mean that it can't be changed from time to time for unusual events. Therefore, there needs to be some room for flexibility in your routines.

Daily Plan

Here is an example of a regular daily plan (the individual events are described in further detail in this chapter):

7:00 A.M.	Arrive, play with blocks or other toys
7:30 A.M.	Eat breakfast
8:00 A.M.	Watch educational television
8:30 A.M.	Do arts and crafts at the table (paint with water, color, use Play-Doh)
9:00 A.M.	Preschool time or circle time (i.e., lesson, flannelboard stories, music, alphabet and number learning)
9:30 A.M.	Do a craft that goes with the lesson
9:45 A.M.	Diaper-changing time
9:50 A.M.	Snack
10:00 A.M.	Toy time, outdoor play, or bicycle time
10:30 A.M.	Dance to music, child aerobics, or music time
10:45 A.M.	Movie time (have the children select and view a video while provider prepares lunch)
11:10 A.M.	Wash hands
11:15 A.M.	Lunch
11:45 A.M.	Diaper-changing time
11:50 A.M.	Play outdoors
12:05 P.M.	Story time (a child chooses a story) or movie time
12:15 P.M.	Nap time
2:15 P.M.	Diaper-changing time
2:20 P.M.	Snack
2:30 P.M.	Play outdoors
3:00 P.M.	Do fun work for prizes
4:00 P.M.	Game time; or alphabet, number, color, or shapes flashcards
4:30 P.M.	Free play outdoors or take a walk
4:45 P.M.	Diaper-changing time and wash-up time
5:00 P.M.	Watch educational TV or listen to a cassette book and tape while provider vacuums the floor
5:30 P.M.	Children are picked up by parents

If you have infants, their feeding and napping will need to be worked into your schedule.

Preschool or Circle Time

If you subscribe to a preschool program you will have all of the lessons prepared for you. I have used the Kapers for Kids preschool program and am impressed by the quality of the lessons. A list of some of the preschool programs you can subscribe to is referenced on page 127. Most preschool programs include: flannelboard stories, music books and tapes, crafts (instructions and supplies precut and ready to make), nature/science lessons, language arts, party activities, identification of fun foods, games, and lesson themes. These mail-order kits can be ordered monthly. Store the flannelboard pictures for each story or lesson in a labeled 9" x 12" manila envelope. These envelopes can be alphabetically filed in your day-care filing cabinet. Also file music books, curriculum guides, newsletters, and pattern books in your files.

If you find that you cannot afford these kits every month, Kapers for Kids has introduced a new option for purchasing the program called Funsteps to Learning. This is a 12-day program which allows you to supplement the month's curriculum with your own lessons. The 12-day program will cost you about half the price of the full program. You also have the option of only purchasing the craft patterns and curriculum guide. Curriculum guides, flannelboard stories, craft patterns, and music books and tapes are all reusable.

You can identify and use your own resources in developing preschool lesson plans. Additional resources such as alphabet flashcards and work papers (letters, numbers, colors, shapes) can be purchased from an educational supply or discount store. Circle-time lesson books can be purchased through catalogs or obtained from your local city public library or day-care toy lending library (refer to page 131).

Weekly Themes

If you do not subscribe to a ready-made preschool kit, you may wish to formulate your own weekly or monthly themes. You may include in these weekly or monthly plans: language arts, music and drama, math and science, physical activity, arts and crafts, games, and snacks and cooking. At the beginning of each week or month, compile a list of materials that you will need. Purchase these items and complete any required drawing, cutting, or assembling in advance so that you are prepared for the week. You may want to prepare a monthly calendar which identifies all of the activities included in that month's curriculum, and a bulletin board displaying the week's or month's theme. Store all lesson preparation and plan materials in your filing cabinet. Share the curriculum plans or calendar with interested parents so that they can be made aware of what their children are learning at your preschool. The following are examples of weekly theme ideas, including lesson plans and materials needed:

Theme One: Zoo Animals

Materials needed:

Snacks

- peanuts
- bananas
- hot dogs or Vienna sausages
- alfalfa sprouts
- animal crackers
- animal-shaped fruit snacks.
- two slices of bread for each child
- one slice of bologna for each child
- one slice of cheese for each child
- raisins
- pancake batter

Arts and Crafts/Lesson Preparation

- pictures of zoo animals
- magazines and coloring books
- poster board
- map of the world

- large cardboard zoo animal with holes for bean bag toss
- bean bags
- Play-Doh
- scissors, glue, stapler, hole punch, and paste
- note asking children to bring stuffed zoo animals on Wednesday
- book *Lyle, the Crocodile* by Bernard Waber
- book *The Great Zoo Hunt!* by Pippa Unwin
- music tape
- white ricrac
- brads
- green construction paper
- drawing of an outline of a zebra for each child
- paper plates (two for each child)
- one copy of zoo animal pictures for each child (refer to pages 149 and 150)
- string or yarn

Monday

Language Arts   Make a collection of zoo animal pictures found in magazines, coloring books, and the like and show these to the children. Have them name the animals.

Music and Drama   Finger Play

Five Little Monkeys

Five little monkeys jumping on the bed
  (*Have your hand with all five fingers move up and down*)
One fell off and broke his head
  (*Point one finger down then point to your head*)
Mama called the doctor and the doctor said
  (*Pretend to dial a phone and listen on a receiver*)
"No more monkeys jumping on the bed!"
  (*Shake your head for "no" and shake your finger*)

Continue with four, three, two, and one little monkey until there are no more monkeys.

Math and Science   Look at the pictures of the zoo animals. Have the children count how many legs each animal has. Describe the animals to the children. Teach them about each animal (what they eat, sleeping habits, where they live).

Physical Activity   Show the children the pictures of the zoo animals and have them move like the animal and make the sounds the animal makes.

Arts and Crafts   Have the children cut out of coloring books or magazines, pictures of animals that belong in a zoo. Provide each child with some poster board to glue or paste the pictures on in making their own zoo animal collage.

Snack   Serve a variety of foods that zoo animals eat and have the children guess which animal eats which food(s). For example:

- elephant—peanuts
- monkey—bananas
- lion—meat (Vienna sausage or hot dog)
- giraffe—grass (alfalfa sprouts)

Tuesday

Language Arts   Read the book *The Great Zoo Hunt!* by Pippa Unwin, which can be borrowed out from your local public library.

Music and Drama   Have the children, one at a time, act out a zoo animal and have the rest of the children guess what animal it is.

Math and Science   Obtain a map of the world. Place the zoo animals on the map in each country the animal is from. (Do some research from encyclopedias or other books.)

Physical Activity   Make a large zoo animal cut out of cardboard with holes to throw bean bags through. Have a bean bag toss.

Arts and Crafts   Have the children shape Play-Doh into zoo animals. Put the animals on display.

Snack   Serve animal crackers

Wednesday

Language Arts   Learn about the letter "Z". Learn that zoo starts with the letter "Z". Have the children practice saying and writing the letter.

Music and Drama   Sing a song about a zoo animal.

Math and Science   Have the children bring stuffed animals that can be found in a zoo, such as bears, lions, tigers, crocodiles, giraffes, birds, snakes. Line the stuffed animals in a row and count them together. Then see how many animals you have if you take one or two away or how many you have if you add one or two.

Physical Activity   Take your stuffed zoo animals for a walk.

Arts and Crafts   Provide the children with an outline of a zebra. Let them color stripes on it.

Snack   Give each child two slices of bread cut into circles (trim of excess), a piece of bologna, raisins, and a slice of cheese. Have the children create a zoo animal shape of their choice out of these items.

Thursday

Language Arts

The Turtle

The turtle crawls on the ground,
And makes a rustling sound.
He carries his house wherever he goes,
And when he is scared
He pulls in his nose
and covers his toes.

Author Unknown

Arts and Crafts   Make a "Zoo Animals" holder (a pocket folder) for zoo animal pictures. The pattern and corresponding instructions can be found on pages 149 and 150.

Physical Activity   Learn about fast and slow by running fast like fast zoo animals and moving slow like slow zoo animals. Teach the children which zoo animals run quickly and which move slowly.

Game   Sort the animal pictures from the arts and crafts activity into various categories (e.g., jungle animals, mountain animals, birds, reptiles, farm animals, water animals).

Snack   Eat zoo animal–shaped fruit snacks.

Friday

Language Arts   Read the book *Lyle, the Crocodile* by Bernard Waber, which can be borrowed from your local public library.

Music and Drama   Play music and move like zoo animals to the music.

Arts and Crafts   Make an alligator (refer to page 151).

Snack   Serve pancakes shaped as zoo animals. Make up some pancake batter and ask each child what zoo animal they would like you to cook for them.

Physical Activity   Have the children play the game "Simon Says." Give out the following commands prefaced by the words, "Simon Says." Trick them by giving a command without saying "Simon Says." Whoever obeys the command without the "Simon Says" before it loses and is out of the game. Play until all children are "out."

   Jump like a kangaroo.
   Climb like a monkey.
   Slither like a snake.
   Run like a cheetah.
   Crawl like a turtle.
   Fly like an eagle.

Theme Two: The Five Senses

Materials needed:

Snacks

- finger food snack
- delicious-smelling snack
- loud crunchy snack
- delicious-looking snack
- delicious-tasting snack

Arts and Crafts/Lesson Preparation

- a copy of "A Touching Book" for each child (refer to pages 152, 153, 154, and 155)
- pennies (two for each child)
- cotton balls (five or six for each child)
- scrap of flannel material for each child
- a piece of sandpaper for each child
- popcorn kernels
- piece of fake fur for each child
- glue
- blindfold
- items to touch
- pictures of things that we can smell
- pictures of different kinds of noses
- "scratch-'n-sniff" stickers
- a sound book
- large construction paper
- Pin the Tail on the Donkey game
- toilet paper roll inserts (two for each child)
- construction paper
- yarn
- white interfacing
- pastels
- permanent marker
- gloss finish (in a spray can)

- copy of Speckled Frog figures (refer to pages 156 and 157)
- pictures of a nose, a hand, eyes, ears, and a tongue
- foods to taste
- poster board
- magazines with pictures of food

Monday—Touch

Language Arts/Arts and Crafts   Make "A Touching Book." Refer to pages 152, 153, 154, and 155.

Game   Blindfold the children and let them touch some items, such as flowers, keys, a spoon, rock, leaf, pencil, and have them guess what the items are by how they feel.

Physical Activity   Play touch tag.

Music and Drama   Sing "Ring Around the Rosies" and hold hands as you go around. Learn that holding hands is using the sense of touch: "Ring around the rosies, a pocket full of posies/Ashes, ashes, we all fall down!"

Snack   Serve popcorn, raisins, or other snacks that the children can eat with their hands.

Tuesday—Smell

Language Arts   Describe different smells (sweet, stale, stinky). Show pictures of things that we can smell (flowers, fire/smoke, popcorn, rain).

Math and Science   Show pictures of different kinds of noses (for instance, elephant trunk, bird beak, people nose, dog snout). Line them up on the flannelboard and count them.

Physical Activity   Take a nature walk and pick and collect flowers or plants that have a unique smell.

Arts and Crafts   Make a book out of the items collected from the nature walk. Glue them into a book titled "Things I Can Smell." Decorate the cover of the book with "scratch-'n-sniff" stickers.

Snack   Serve a delicious-smelling snack, such as freshly baked bread, cookies.

Wednesday—Hearing

Language Arts   Read a sound book. Let the children push the buttons to make the sounds.

Music and Drama   Sing "Do Your Ears Hang Low?"

> Do your ears hang low?
> Do they wobble to and fro?
> Can you tie them in a knot?
> Can you tie them in a bow?
> Can you throw them over your shoulder
> Like a continental soldier?
> Do your ears hang low?

Physical Activity   Take a walk outdoors and have the children see how many different sounds they can hear. Write down the sounds as the children identify them.

Math and Science   Teach the children that deaf people cannot speak. Teach the children a few words in sign language. Teach them that this is how deaf people communicate.

Game—Charades   Children guess which animal is being acted out. The children are instructed not to make any sounds when acting out their animal. Convey to the children that this is what it's like to communicate without use of a sense of hearing.

Arts and Crafts   Roll and staple a large sheet of construction paper into the shape of a megaphone. Explain that the megaphone is used to make our voices louder.

Snack   Eat a loud crunchy snack (potato chips, crackers).

Thursday—Sight

Language Arts   Read some books about eyes which can be borrowed from your local library.

Music and Drama   Have the children pretend to be blind. Blind-fold each child and have them try walking across the room. (Be sure to remove obstacles and potential hazards.) Let them try again with the use of a cane.

Game—Pin the Tail on the Donkey   Explain to the children how their other senses attempt to compensate when they cannot see.

Math and Science   Share information with the children about the human eye. Conduct a mock eye examination using a facsimile of an eye chart.

Arts and Crafts   Make a pair of binoculars. Tape two toilet paper roll inserts together with masking tape. Cover the rolls with colored construction paper. Punch a hole at each end of the binoculars. Fasten yarn to the binoculars so that they can hang from the child's neck. Instruct the children in the use of binoculars.

Snack   Eat something that looks delicious, such as assorted fresh fruit or ice cream sundaes.

Friday—Taste

Language Arts   Share with the children a picture of a nose, eyes, ears, hand, and tongue. Introduce each object as one of our five senses. Say the words together.

Music and Drama   Sing "Five Little Speckled Frogs" which is about frogs eating bugs. If desired, make flannelboard figures (refer to pages 156 and 157) to go along the song.

> Five little speckled frogs
> Sitting on a speckled log
> Eating the most delicious bugs, yum yum!
> One jumped into the pool
> Where it was nice and cool
> Now there are four green speckled frogs, glub, glub!

Continue until there are no green speckled frogs left.

Math and Science   Explain that our tongues provide us with a sense of taste. Pass around a hand mirror and have each child examine his or her tongue.

Game   Blindfold the children and have them sample various foods. Allow the children to identify the foods served.

Arts and Crafts   Have each child make a collage of foods that he or she likes and dislikes. Divide a piece of poster board into two halves, drawing a line in the center. One side of the poster will represent the foods the child likes and the other the foods the child dislikes. Have the children use magazines in finding and cutting out different types of food.

Snack   Serve a delicious tasting snack.

Theme Three: Stories That Teach

Materials needed:

Snacks

- bread dough
- small bread pans
- sugar cookies
- sprinkles
- milk
- parsley
- candy canes
- fresh fruit
- celery
- peanut butter
- pudding

Arts and Crafts/Lesson Preparation

- the following stories: The Little Red Hen, Cinderella, The Shepherd Boy and the Wolf, Little Red Riding Hood, and The Tortoise and the Hare. If you are unfamiliar with any of these stories, they can be obtained from your local public library.

- contact paper
- flannel fabric or self-sticking felt tape
- flannelboard figures (refer to pages 158, 161, 162, 163, 164, and 165) for each of the five stories

Option 1: Figures copied and enlarged, colored, cut out, laminated or covered with clear contact paper (both sides), and flannel fabric glued on the back of each (with fabric glue). Store in a labeled 9" x 12" manila envelope.

Option 2: Figures copied and enlarged, colored, cut out, laminated, or covered with clear contact paper (both sides), and self-sticking felt tape (may be purchased at teaching supply stores) attached to the back of each for use on a flannelboard. Store in a labeled 9" x 12" manila envelope.

Option 3: Figures copied and enlarged, traced onto and cut out of white interfacing, colored with pastels, outlined in permanent black marker, and sprayed with a gloss finish. Store in a labeled 9" x 12" manila envelope.

Option 4: Figures copied and enlarged, colored, laminated or covered with clear contact paper, and a piece of magnetic tape attached to the back of each for use on the refrigerator or a magnetic board.

- flannelboard
- magnetic board or refrigerator
- stuffed animals—dog, cat, duck, pig, or any other animal characters which can be improvised in the telling of the story
- kernels of wheat
- hand wheat grinder (optional)
- bread dough
- brown lunch sacks (one for each child)
- glue
- materials for making a Red Hen for each child (refer to pages 159 and 160 for pattern and items needed)
- cassette tape, record, or CD of a musical version of Cinderella
- music (for ballroom dancing)
- cardboard (cut one 12" x 1" for each child)

- cardboard (cut one star shape for each child)
- glitter
- tin foil
- ten copies of the sheep figure from the Shepherd Boy and the Wolf flannelboard figures (refer to page 164)
- cardboard (cut as sheep)
- cotton balls
- white construction paper
- baskets
- measuring tape
- crayons
- one copy of Little Red Riding Hood flannelboard figures for each child (refer to page 163) to take home
- magnetic tape
- manila envelopes
- ten copies of the tortoise and ten copies of the hare from The Tortoise and the Hare flannelboard figures (refer to page 165) for use in the matching game
- bathroom cups (four for each child)
- paper bowls (one for each child)
- green construction paper
- green paint.
- self-sticking felt tape

Monday

Story: The Little Red Hen
Moral: Hard work brings rewards.

There are also other stories that illustrate the benefits of hard work, such as The Three Little Pigs and The Ant and the Grasshopper. I recognized the need of teaching children the value of work as I observed the behavior of a few of my day care children. Such tasks as picking up toys, finishing a drawing, and completing jigsaw puzzles were very difficult for some of the children. In today's world of videos, television, and Nintendo, children may not learn to apply themselves when completing constructive tasks. Many mothers of preschool and grade-school children are run ragged trying to keep up with the additional work created by their own children. However, children are far more capable than we give them credit for. They can help out around the house. Not that we should go back to the days of child labor, but children should be able to complete a list of chores and clean up after themselves. Through experience, children can learn that work itself can be rewarding and fun!

Language Arts   Present the flannelboard story of The Little Red Hen. If you have stuffed animals or puppets of these characters, you may want to use them to illustrate the story.

Music and Drama   Have a skit of The Little Red Hen. Assign each child a character to act out. If desired, dress up as the characters and present the skit in front of an audience or video-tape your skit.

Math and Science   Learn how bread is made. Start with kernels of wheat. Grind the wheat into flour if you can obtain a hand wheat grinder. Let the children take turns grinding the wheat into flour. Have some bread dough available and let the children knead the dough, put it into small loaf pans, and put it in the oven after the dough has risen.

Physical Activity   Act out the Little Red Hen's chores.

Arts and Crafts   Make a Little Red Hen (refer to pages 159 and 160).

Snack and Cooking   Bake the small loaves of bread which were prepared as the science activity and eat them for snack.

Tuesday

Story: Cinderella
Moral: Life has hard times, but dreams can come true.

Language Arts   Present the flannelboard story of Cinderella (refer to pages 161 and 162).

Music and Drama   Sing songs from Disney's *Cinderella* or another musical version of *Cinderella*.

Math and Science   Ask the children to identify how many pairs or twos are in the story of Cinderella. Example: two glass slippers, two stepsisters, the prince and Cinderella, and the number 2 in 12:00, midnight.

Physical Activity   Play some music and pretend to be dancing at a ball.

Arts and Crafts   Make a magic wand. Items needed include the following: cardboard, tin foil, and glitter. Cut out a 12" x 1" strip of cardboard. Cut out a star shape. Glue or staple together. Cover with tin foil. Glue glitter on the star.

Snack   Eat sugar cookies with sprinkles on top. Serve milk.

Wednesday

Story: The Shepherd Boy and the Wolf
Moral: People will not believe the liar.

Language Arts   Present the flannelboard story of The Shepherd Boy and the Wolf (refer to page 164).

Music and Drama   Let the children act out the story taking turns playing the role of the sheep, wolf, and people.

Math and Science   Count sheep. In advance, copy ten of the sheep (refer to page 164). Cut out and cover figures with contact paper and back with flannel fabric or self-sticking felt tape. Place the figures on the flannelboard and take turns having each child count how many sheep you have up on the board.

Physical Activity   Play outdoors the game, Wolf and Sheep Tag, in which all of the children but one are sheep. Let the wolf chase the sheep and tag them. When tagged, a sheep must lie down. Play until all of the sheep are down. Choose another child to be the wolf.

Arts and Crafts   Make a sheep using the sheep flannelboard figure pattern. Cut one out of cardboard for each child (enlarge, if desired). Let the children glue cotton balls onto their sheep. Draw and cut out eyes and a mouth from construction paper and glue on the face.

Movie   Show the movie *Pinocchio*, which represents another story about telling the truth.

Snack   Pretend to eat grass (parsley) like a sheep along with the regular snack. For a treat, if possible, serve a candy cane to represent a shepherd's cane.

Thursday

Story: Little Red Riding Hood
Moral: Obey your parents. Don't talk to strangers.

Language Arts   Present the flannelboard story of Little Red Riding Hood (refer to page 163).

Music and Drama   Carry baskets and skip to music. Pretend to go to Grandma's house.

Math and Science   Using a measuring tape, measure the distance from home to Grandma's house (one side of the room to the other). Teach the children about units of measurement (inches and feet, centimeters and meters).

Physical Activity   Skip to Grandma's house. Hop to Grandma's house. Walk to Grandma's house. Run to Grandma's house.

Arts and Crafts   Children enjoy telling flannelboard stories. Make a copy of the flannelboard characters for each child. Let them color the figures, and laminate or cover both sides of each one with contact paper. Place a strip of magnetic tape on the back of each figure and provide each child with a manila envelope to keep their flannelboard characters in. At home the children can place their figures on the refrigerator.

Cooking and Snack   Have the children make fruit baskets by placing fresh fruit in a hollowed-out half of an orange. Eat for snack.

Friday

Story: The Tortoise and the Hare by Aesop
Moral: Slow and steady wins the race.

The story helps teach children to keep trying and not to give up. They don't have to be the fastest, strongest, prettiest, or smartest to succeed.

Language Arts Using the flannelboard, share the story of The Tortoise and the Hare (refer to page 165).

Music and Drama Have the children act out the story of The Tortoise and the Hare, taking turns playing the part of these two characters.

Physical Activity Run like rabbits, move like turtles.

Math and Science Look up tortoises and hares in the encyclopedia. Help the children to learn what they eat, where they live, how fast they run, etc.

Game—Match Copy ten each of the tortoise and the hare from the flannelboard figure pattern on page 165. Color the figures and cover with contact paper or laminate. Play the game like the game Concentration. Have each child take turns turning two cards over in an attempt to find a match. Since there are only two different characters to match, it is a good way to teach the younger children how to play games.

Arts and Crafts Make a turtle. Items needed: bathroom-size paper cups (four for each child), paper bowl, green construction paper, black marker, and green paint. Have the children paint the bottom of the bowl green. Put glue on the bottom of the four bathroom-size paper cups. Press the cups to the unpainted side of the bowl—on the bowl's rim. Out of green construction paper, cut out a head shape. In black marker, draw eyes and mouth on the head. Glue the head to the unpainted rim of the bowl. Cut out a tail from green construction paper. Glue the tail to the other end (unpainted side) of the bowl.

Snack   Help the children to understand the concepts of fast and slow (like the tortoise and the hare) by eating a snack that can be eaten quickly, such as pudding, and one that takes time, such as celery with peanut butter.

Theme Four: Good Health Habits

Materials needed:

Snacks

- apples
- any healthy snack
- finger food
- Gatorade
- trail mix
- milk
- cookies

Arts and Crafts/Lesson Preparation

- books from library about teeth, nutrition, germs and sickness, rest, and exercise
- a picture of a mouth with twenty teeth
- paper
- crayons
- child-size scissors, glue
- small award charts (one for each child)
- award stickers
- small toothpastes (one for each child)
- construction paper
- magazines
- small soap for each child
- Disney or other character liquid soap
- child aerobics video tape
- soft ball or jump rope for each child

Before Monday morning make and hang up on a bulletin board or wall the following pictures: a child brushing his or her teeth, eating good food, washing his or her hands, sleeping, exercising, and bathing.

Monday—Brushing Teeth

Language Arts   Read to the children books from the local library about teeth.

Music and Drama   Have the children act out an appointment with the dentist.

Math and Science   Referring to a picture of a mouth with twenty teeth, count the teeth.

Physical Activity   Have the children pretend to brush teeth.

Arts and Crafts   Make a toothbrush. Draw a toothbrush for each child. Have the children color the toothbrushes and cut them out. Cut slits to make bristles.

Snack   Have the children eat healthy snacks for their teeth, such as apples, milk, and the like.

Homework   Give each child a small awards chart with twenty squares (these can be found in teaching supply stores). Provide each child with twenty small stickers for the chart. Tell the children to place a sticker on their charts each time they brush their teeth. As a reward, present each child with a small child's-size toothpaste for completing his or her chart.

Tuesday—Eat Healthy Food

Language Arts   Cut out pictures of different foods from magazines. Laminate or cover the pictures with contact paper and back with flannel fabric (using fabric glue) or self-sticking felt tape. Distribute the food pictures to the children. Divide the flannelboard up into the four food groups. Have each child come up, one at a time, and place his or her food item on the flannelboard under the appropriate food category.

Math and Science   Teach the children about eating healthy and how diet affects the human body.

Refer to library books in preparing for this lesson.

Physical Activity   Have one child leave the room while you hide pictures of various kinds of foods. Invite the child back into the room and have him or her find and identify all the pictures. Repeat for each child.

Arts and Crafts   Make a collage of foods on large construction paper. Provide the children with child-size scissors. Let them cut out of magazines, pictures of healthy foods and pictures of not so healthy foods. Divide the collage into the two sections.

Snack   Serve a healthy snack.

Wednesday—Wash Hands Before Eating

Language Arts   Find books from the library that provide information and illustrations on personal hygiene (washing hands, germs). Teach the children that washing their hands before eating helps keep them healthy.

Music and Drama   Have the children act out how to wash their hands appropriately.

Physical Activity   Go to the sink and line the children up. Have each child wash his or her hands. Teach the children how to wash their hands with soap and dry them.

Arts and Crafts   Provide the children with a small motel-size bar of soap. Let each child draw a shape on his or her soap. Carve each child's shape out of the soap.

Snack   Have the children wash their hands and then eat a finger food for a snack.

Homework   Give each child another small chart with twenty squares and twenty stickers. Have the children place a sticker on the chart each time they wash their hands. (Send the chart home with each child along with a note soliciting the parent's support.) As a reward, provide each child with a Disney or other character-shaped bottle of liquid soap.

Thursday—Exercise

Language Arts Teach the children the importance of getting enough rest and exercise. If possible, find and share fictional stories on the subject.

Music and Drama Have the children dance to a child aerobics tape.

Math and Science Teach the children about the different things that we can do to exercise. Write the children's ideas on a chalkboard. Have the children count the number of items listed.

Physical Activity Have relay races outdoors.

Arts and Crafts Have the children make a collage of magazine pictures illustrating different forms of physical exercise and activity, such as running, basketball, soccer, football, bicycling, roller skating, and so on.

Snack Have the children eat trail mix and drink a sports drink (Gatorade).

Homework Have the children fill out a small awards chart for exercising every day. As a reward, provide each child with a soft ball or jump rope upon completion of the chart.

Friday—Rest

Language Arts Explain to the children how the body requires sleep.

Music and Drama Play house and pretend it is bedtime by turning out the lights and having the children lie down quietly as if they were sleeping. Play lullaby music.

Math and Science Have the children look at a clock as you show them the time most people go to bed at night and the time most people get up in the morning.

Physical Activity Play some music and let the children dance around. Stop the music and have the children lie down and rest. Repeat as many times as desired.

Arts and Crafts   Have each child draw a picture of the room in his or her house where he or she sleeps.

Snack   Serve milk and cookies (a bedtime snack).

Activities

Toy Time

At my day care we call it toy time when the children go in the toy room and have free play with the toys. They can choose one box of toys at a time, return it, and get another one, or they can play with the toys from the toy box. When toy time is over we have clean-up time before proceeding with the next activity. We sing the clean-up song as we return the toys to the toy box. Sometimes I allow one child to be the leader (maybe the child of the day) and let that child be in charge of telling the other children to put the toys away.

Outdoor Play

Outdoor play may include activity with the swing set, sand box, balls, playhouse, tricycles, etc.

Nap Time

Children who require naps should sleep well if they are on a regular routine. A good lunch and exercise during the day can help. Darken the room at nap time. I prefer to have nap time fairly early, around 12:00 or 12:30 P.M. until 2:00 or 2:30 P.M., so that the children will sleep well for their parents at night. Most parents want their children to have a nap so that they are not irritable at dinner or fall asleep too early. However, parents do not appreciate naps too late in the afternoon because in the evening their children are less likely to go to sleep at their usual time. Some children have outgrown naps. These children can rest for twenty to thirty minutes and then get up and do something quietly until nap time is over. Some children are at the stage of taking naps occasionally, but do not need a nap every day. The parents may appreciate it if you tell them whether or not their child has napped that day so that they know what time to put their child to bed at night.

It is preferable to have all the older children together for nap time in the same room. Infants in cribs (who don't climb out yet) may be in a separate room. When I first began my day-care business, I allowed the children to nap in separate rooms. One day I went to check on a five-year-old girl and found her beginning to stick an object into an electrical outlet. This is why, from my perspective, there is a need to keep all of the day-care children together in full view during nap time.

Nap time is an excellent time for you to enjoy some quiet time during the middle of the day.

Bicycle Time

Bicycle time is a specific time in which you watch the children ride tricycles, bicycles, scooters, cars, or power cars. The activity provides the children with some good physical exercise. Perhaps you have a large cement patio or circular area in your front driveway that is good for riding bicycles. If not, even lawn or dirt will suffice.

Dance Time

Play a cassette tape, CD, or record of children's music and have the children dance to the music. It's great exercise. This activity is especially good on cold or rainy days when the children are unable to go outside.

Kid Aerobics

Create your own exercise routine to music or buy a children's aerobics tape such as *Mousercise* by Disney. The workout represents a great way of letting the children get their energy out. You may wish to reward those who complete the workout with a prize from the prize bucket or add some stickers to their awards chart.

Music Time

Play the piano or cassette tape/CD or sing a cappella with the children. You can use creative ways of choosing songs, such as fishing for fishes with songs written on the back (that is, selecting paper cutouts of fishes with magnetic tape, using a pole with a string and magnet attached). Kids love to fish and love to lead the music, too. You may use hand motions or flannelboard pictures with your songs.

Movie Time

You can purchase videos from time to time to add to your collection (such as Disney features and other animated films). You may also want to consider renting videos or checking them out from your local library (refer to pages 127 and 128). Allow a child to select the video (for instance, a child who has behaved well or your child of the day).

Story Time

You may have many children's books and magazines of your own or you may choose to check some out from your local library. You can line the books up on the floor and let a child who is sitting quietly choose the book you will read.

Fun Work for Prizes

Fun work for prizes is especially good for older children after school to keep them busy and learning. Have puzzles, school work papers, educational computer programs (if you have a computer for your day care), crossword puzzles, dot to dots, and other activities available. Have a large chart with each child's name on it and squares by each name for the placement of stickers. These charts can be purchased at your local teaching supply store. On most charts, there are twenty to twenty-three squares in a row.

Another way of using the chart is to laminate the chart and use an erasable marker to write the children's names and for placing check marks in the squares. When full, this chart can be erased and reused.

Have a set number of stickers to award for each project such as: 60-piece puzzle—5 stickers, 100-piece puzzle—10 stickers, educational computer program—2 stickers, work papers—2 stickers, crossword puzzles—5 stickers, etc.

When the child completes a row, he or she can pick a prize out of the prize bucket and begin a new row.

Game Time   Play games with the children during game time. Not only are games fun, but they teach children many things, such as following rules, dealing with competition, having patience, the skills of mathematics and reading, etc. Some excellent children's games are outlined on page 129.

Walk Time   Take the children on a walk around the neighborhood. Teach them about safety in crossing streets. Teach the children about nature as you observe and examine birds, insects, and various forms of vegetation.

Picnic Time   Just for fun, eat some of your lunches outdoors on a blanket or at a picnic table.

Swim Time   In the summer, you may wish to let the children play in a wading pool or in the sprinklers. This activity requires constant and close supervision, and parental permission.

Pizza Party   Order pizza for fun. It can be fun for the children to have a combined pool and pizza party. Or have the children make their own pizzas. You can use refrigerated biscuit dough and let the children put on their own toppings. Invite a neighbor friend and her children to join you for the party.

Bubbles   You can purchase bubbles and bubble wands for the children. Or you can improvise by using dish soap and water for a solution, and fly swatters as bubble wands.

Water Balloons

Children like to play with water balloons. Children may use the balloons to play catch, toss them and watch them splash, or just hold them in enjoying their unique feel. Be sure to clean up the remains so small children won't try to swallow and possibly choke on the balloon fragments.

Restaurant

Play restaurant. First have the children make their own menus. Create a trifold which resembles a menu out of a large (12" x 18") sheet of construction paper. Have the children cut out pictures of foods from magazines and glue them on their menus. Write a price (e.g., $5.99) by each menu item. Have one child be the waiter. Use a small child's table and play dishes. You may want to use real food and play restaurant at lunch or snack time. If you cover the menus with clear contact paper, they can be used over and over again.

Carnival

Parents should be notified about the carnival and that the cost will be 50 cents or $1.00, for example. The money will help the day-care provider with the cost of the items. Set up booths (i.e., designated areas in the yard) and have a carnival. You can purchase tickets at an office supply store or at some discount stores. Your carnival could include the following booths: ticket, ring toss, fishpond, popcorn, hot dogs, lemonade, bowling, and bean bag toss. You may wish to charge 10 cents per ticket and in the exchange of money for tickets, teach children about using money. Send out flyers in advance so that the parents can provide their child with some money that day.

Book Talk

Have each child bring their favorite book from home. Read the books the children have brought from home and serve cookies and lemonade. Send out flyers announcing this event.

Rodeo

Have events such as steer roping (i.e., toss a rope with a lasso over a post or other object), barrel racing (i.e., make an obstacle course—use pretend stick horses), and other events. Have one child dress up as a clown and have the other children dress up as cowboys.

Movie Theater

Serve popcorn, collect tickets, close the curtains, turn out the lights and watch a movie.

Movie-Making Day

If you have a camcorder, tape a typical day at your day-care home. Make copies of the tape for parents to keep so they can see what their children do during the day, and the children can watch themselves at home. The parents will appreciate having a memorable video tape of their children at that preschool age.

Color Day

Have a specific color day. Each child wears clothes of that color and brings a food or snack of that color. Have the children identify other items of the same color.

Puppet Theater

Put on a puppet show. Purchase puppets, check them out from your local library or toy lending library, or have the children make them.

Diaper-Changing Time

You may choose to have specific diaper-changing times when you diaper all of the children. This helps you not to forget to diaper a child. You can diaper children between times as needed.

Ice Cream Party

Let the children make their own ice cream sundaes. Have different kinds of toppings (e.g., nuts, coconut, M&Ms, jelly, chocolate syrup, cherries, other candies, marshmallows) for the children to use in making their own sundaes.

Car Wash Day

Have children bring their own bicycles, cars, or tricycles (or use your own). Have the children use the hose, soap, spray bottles, towels, in washing their riding toys.

Dress-up Day

Let the children play dress-up by wearing your old clothes, shoes, and hats. You can also purchase Halloween costumes at a discount after the holiday for use in dress-up.

Painting Day

Announce this day with a flyer and have the children wear old clothes or paint shirts. Plaster of Paris figures are fun to paint. The children also enjoy finger-painting, watercolors, and paint with water books.

Olympics

Have a track and field day with the following events: running races, long jump, relays, and Frisbee throw. Present ribbons for first, second, and third places.

Camping Day

Set up a tent in your yard and have a pretend campout. Have the children use their imaginations in having a play hike, camp-fire, and picnic. Pretend to go fishing with poles made from sticks and boating with boats made from boxes.

Homemade Toys and Learning Materials:
Toys From Trash and Scraps

The following items are primarily intended for use at your day care. However, some of the items can be made by the children to take home.

Milk Carton Blocks

The following items are required: several empty half-gallon milk cartons and decorative contact paper.

These are nice big lightweight building blocks. Children can use them in building a little house or tall tower. The children also enjoy knocking the structures down. Although large, these blocks can be stored in a trash can or bag in the garage. As with any toy, the children should return the blocks when they are through playing with them. If left out, the blocks can easily get stepped on and bent out of shape.

Instructions for assembly of blocks:

1. Open the milk carton openings all of the way.
2. Wash and dry the inside of each carton.
3. With open ends together, put one milk carton inside the other.
4. To decorate, cover with decorative contact paper.

Milk Cap ABCs

The following items are required: milk caps and permanent marker.

Save the caps from milk gallon jugs. Write the letters of the alphabet on them in permanent marker. Have the children identify the letters. Let the children hold the letters they get right and count them at the end of the game.

Bean Bags

The following items are required: small amount of fabric and uncooked dried beans.

Instructions for assembly of bean bags:

1. Cut fabric into two squares the desired size and shape of your bean bag.
2. Put the "right" sides of the fabric together face to face, then sew the perimeter of the bag, leaving 5/8" from the edge and enough room for turning the bag right side out.
3. Turn right sides out.

4. Fill the bag with beans.
5. Hand-stitch the opening.

Play-Doh

The following items are required:

- 4 cups flour
- 8 tablespoons cream of tartar
- 2 cups salt
- ½ cup oil
- 4 cups water
- food coloring

Instructions for making dough:

1. Combine all the ingredients in the order listed.
2. Cook over low heat until it becomes stiff and hard to stir.
3. Turn out on a board and knead the dough until it smoothes out easily.

Capes

Children love to wear capes and run around pretending to be superheroes. Select your desired color: black for Batman, red for Superman, and pink for a princess.

The following items are required:

- stretch fabric (enough for each cape)
- scissors
- thread and needle or sewing machine

Instructions for making capes:

1. Cut out a cape shape approximately 28″ wide x 23″ long.
2. Cut out the tie approximately 32″ long x 1″ wide. Fold over the "right" sides together and sew. Turn right side out.
3. Sew tie onto cape at the top.

Pom-poms

Children love to shake pom-poms as they skip, run, or march to music. The following items are required: newspaper and masking tape.

Instructions for making poms-poms:

1. Cut the newspaper into several long thin strips.
2. Gather the strips together.
3. Tape the strips together in the center.
4. Fold the strips over and bind the folded end with masking tape (several layers).

Felt Dolls

Children enjoy dressing this little felt doll.

The following items are required: felt squares (different colors), thin-lined permanent marker, and scissors.

Instructions for making felt dolls:

1. Cut out a doll of white or skin-colored felt approximately 10" high.
2. Draw a face on the doll with the permanent marker.
3. Cut out different styles of hair from yellow, red, brown, and black felt.
4. Cut out clothes to fit the doll from different colors of felt.
5. Use a full piece of felt to make a carrying bag for doll and clothes. Fold the felt square as you would a business letter (i.e., bottom side up and then top side down). Sew on a snap to keep closed.

Flannelboard Figures

The following items are required: pictures, clear contact paper, fabric glue, flannel fabric, white interfacing, black marker, pastels, spray gloss finish, self-sticking felt tape, and felt.

You can make your own flannelboard figures by cutting pictures out from magazines, coloring books, or other sources. Color the figures if necessary. To protect the surface of the figures, cover with clear contact paper or laminate. Glue flannel fabric to the back (with fabric glue) or attach self-sticking felt tape.

Another way to make flannelboard figures is by tracing the

picture onto white interfacing. The figure is outlined in black marker and colored with pastels. Spray with glossy finish and cut out the figure.

If your flannelboard figures consist of shapes without a lot of detail, you may want to cut the figures out from felt.

Refrigerator or Magnetic Board Figures

The following items are required: pictures, clear contact paper, and a roll of magnetic tape.

Instructions for making refrigerator or magnetic board figures:

1. Find the pictures you want to use.
2. Color figures, if needed.
3. Cover the figures with clear contact paper or laminate .
4. Attach a strip of magnetic tape (may be purchased from a craft store) to the back of each figure.
5. Use on the refrigerator or magnetic board.

Newspaper Hat

The following items are required: newspaper, clear mailing tape, and decorations such as feathers, lace, sequins, etc.

Make the hat by placing large sheets of newspaper (as thick as desired) around each child's head, and tape around the hat with clear mailing tape. Decorate with whatever you have on hand.

Frisbee

The following items are required: two paper plates, a stapler, and crayons.

Have the children color two paper plates. Staple the top sides of the two paper plates together—top sides facing each other. (This kind of Frisbee won't break a window.)

Crown

The following items are required: empty rinsed bleach bottle and decorations, such as buttons, sequins, and glitter.

Cut a crown shape out of the bleach bottle. Decorate.

Sock Puppet

The following items are required: long sock, craft eyes (available at craft stores), and red felt.

Sew eyes and a piece of red felt for a tongue on the long sock.

Foam Shapes

The following items are required: sponges and milk jug lids.

Cut shapes out of sponges (e.g., square, triangle, circle). Glue the milk jug lid to the sponge to serve as a handle. The foam shapes can be dipped in paint and applied to paper.

Cereal Box Games

The following items are required: games from the back of cereal boxes, clear contact paper, and wipe-off crayons or markers.

Cut out games from the back of cereal boxes (for example, hidden pictures, crossword puzzles). Laminate or cover each game with clear contact paper. Provide the children with wipe-off crayons or markers. The game can be reused by wiping off the crayon or marker.

Surprise Snake

The following items are required: empty Play-Doh container, large construction paper (12″ x 18″), stapler, glue, and colored markers.

Instructions for making a surprise snake:

1. Cut the construction paper into a 6′ strip about 1″ wide (attach four 1½′ strips).
2. Have the children fold the strip in an accordion style.
3. Make another strip the same length as the first strip.
4. Weave the second strip, accordion style, into the first strip.
5. Staple the ends of the two strips together.
6. Cut out a snake head from construction paper.

7. Using colored markers, draw a face on the snake head.
8. Glue the head to one end of the two weaved strips.
9. Press the snake into a Play-Doh container and put the lid on. When the lid is opened, a snake jumps out.

Rhythm Instruments

Drum: Use an empty oatmeal box for the drum. For drumsticks attach empty thread spools to the ends of unsharpened pencils.

Shakers: Fill an empty toilet paper insert with dried beans. Cover the ends with mailing tape.

Cymbals: Use two pan lids.

Tambourine: Cut out the bottom of an oatmeal box (about 1" up from the bottom). Cut two holes in either side. Thread bells on a string and move the bells to the center of the string. Thread each end of the string through one of the two holes and tie the ends in a knot. Trim the ends of the string.

5

Holiday Activities and Crafts

Valentine's Day

Cake Decorating Contest

Items needed: small heart-shaped cakes, icing, award ribbons, and decorations.

Purchase small heart-shaped cake pans and make a valentine cake for each child. Have the older children frost their cakes with pink icing. Have all children decorate their own cakes. Let each child use a decorator tube of icing in adding their own personal touch. Provide each child with a variety of candy, sprinkles, coconut, and other toppings. When finished, line the cakes up on the table for judging. Present every child with an award ribbon. Awards may include: Most Beautiful, Most Delicious, Most Creative, Most Original, etc. Have the children take their cakes home at the end of the day (refer to page 148).

Valentine Stamps

Items needed: paper, scissors, crayons or markers, and glue.

Draw pretend postage stamps with valentine designs. Have the children color and cut out the stamps. The children then glue the stamps to the envelopes of valentines that they will distribute on Valentine's Day.

Valentine Mailboxes

Items needed: boxes, construction paper, scissors, and decorations.

Have each child bring a box from home or collect some yourself. Cover them with colored pink or red construction paper and have the children decorate them. Cut a slot in the box for valentines. Label them with each child's name and save them in your facility until the holiday. On the day of the party, the children can distribute their valentines by placing one in each other child's mailbox. At the end of the day, the children can take their boxes home.

Music

Sing Valentine's Day songs ("Love Is a Hug" and "Valentine Hearts" both by Bev Greene, from *Kapers for Kids*). These holiday songs can be practiced all month and then sung on the day of the party before distributing the valentines.

Story Time

Read books about Valentine's Day. You can borrow these from your local library. Try *Little Mouse's Valentine* by Dave Ross, *How Spider Saved Valentine's Day* by Robert Kraus, and *Valentine for a Dragon* by Shirley Rousseau Murphy.

Decorating

Decorate your day-care facility with Valentine's Day decorations. You can teach the children how to cut out heart shapes and tape them on the walls of your place.

Valentines

Have the children make valentines for family members out of

materials such as lace doilies, construction paper, valentine's stickers, and glitter. Help the children cut out the hearts.

Valentine Rabbit

Refer to pages 166 and 167 for Valentine Rabbit pattern and instructions.

Saint Patrick's Day

I Like Green Day

Teach the children about the color green. Have the children wear green clothes and bring a green snack to share, and learn about things that are green (trees, grass, emeralds, caterpillars).

Story Time

Read a book from your local library about Saint Patrick's Day, such as *Jeremy Bean's St. Patrick's Day* by Alice Schertle, *Patrick's Day* by Elizabeth Lee O'Donnell, and *Mary McLean and the St. Patrick's Day Parade* by Steven Kroll.

Treasure Hunt

Have a treasure hunt using pictures that direct the children to the next clue. These pictures can be cut from magazines and covered with clear contact paper. Save them in a 9″ x 12″ manila envelope and file for use the following year. These pictures may include: a refrigerator, high chair, lamp, washer or dryer, toilet, crib, TV set, and rocking horse. Finish the hunt with a pot of gold at the end of the rainbow (a bag of chocolate gold coins—one coin for each child).

Nature Walk

Go on a nature walk and look for four-leaf clovers.

Decorating

Decorate your day-care space for Saint Patrick's Day with green shamrocks, green balloons, green streamers, and so on. Have the children cut shamrocks out of green construction paper and tape them on the walls.

Easter

Dye Eggs

Have the children color hard-boiled eggs using a store-bought Easter egg kit.

Rabbit Sack

Refer to page 168 for Rabbit Sack pattern and instructions. Place grass and eggs inside the sack.

Easter Egg Hunt

Fill plastic eggs with surprises (toys or candy) and hide them in the house or yard for the children to find and take home.

Music

Sing Easter songs, such as "All Bunnies Have Pink Shiny Noses" and "Little Bunny" by Bev Greene, both from *Kapers for Kids*. Write the titles of the songs on slips of paper and place inside plastic Easter eggs. The children can then pick a song by selecting an egg.

Movie Time

View *Here Comes Peter Cottontail*, *It's the Easter Beagle, Charlie Brown*, or another Easter favorite.

Animals

If you have a pet rabbit, ducks, or chickens, show them to the children. Otherwise, plan a trip to a farm, petting zoo, or pet shop to show the children some of these animals.

Plaster of Paris Refrigerator Magnets

Items needed: Easter candy mold, plaster of Paris, and magnetic tape.

Purchase an Easter candy mold at your local craft store (a mold for making chocolate suckers), but instead of filling with chocolate, fill with plaster of Paris. Don't overfill or the magnets will be too heavy to stay on the refrigerator. Let the children paint them. Glue magnetic tape on the back.

Colors

Teach the children about colors using plastic colored eggs.

Games

Colored Eggs   One child is the wolf and calls out various colors. When the child (a chicken) hears his/her color, he/she tries to run around the tree and back before the wolf (standing a few yards away from the tree) can catch him/her.

Duck, Duck, Goose   One child is "it" and the other children sit in a circle. The child who is "it" calls each child a "duck" as he (or she) walks around the circle touching the head of each child. The child who's "it" chooses a child whom he calls "goose." Then he or she must run from this child around the circle. If he makes it back to this child's place without getting caught, he is safe and the other child is "it," and the game continues. If a child is caught, he must sit in the middle of the circle until someone else who is caught replaces him.

Story Time

Read books about Easter from your local library, such as *The Great Big Especially Beautiful Easter Egg* by James Stevenson, *What a Funny Bunny* by Patricia Whitehead, and *The Chocolate Rabbit* by Maria Claret.

Decorations

Decorate your facility for Easter. Pictures/posters of colored eggs, rabbits, and chickens make for nice decorations.

Math

Have the children guess how many jelly beans are in a jar. The child who guesses the number (or guesses closest to the number) wins. The winner takes the jar of jelly beans home.

Mother's Day

Tissue Paper Carnations

Items needed: tissue paper (any colors desired), stems (green wire stems can be purchased at craft stores), and scissors.

Using six sheets of tissue paper cut out a 6" square. Fold the square accordion style. Twist a green wire stem around the center. Bring up each piece of tissue paper, one at a time to make a carnation. Have children give the carnations to their mothers for Mother's Day.

Paper Holder for Flowers

Items needed: one large sheet of construction paper (12" x 18") for each child.

Shape the construction paper into a cone shape. Staple together. Have the children place their tissue paper carnations in the holder to give to their mothers.

Tissue Paper Corsages

Make a tissue paper carnation. Snip the stem off close to the carnation. Secure pin through the carnation. Place carnation in a box. The corsage may be decorated with leaves, ribbon, etc.

Cereal Necklace

Items needed: flavored cereal like Froot Loops, yarn, and a crayon.

To make the end of the yarn stiff for stringing:

1. Melt a crayon in an old pan on the stove.
2. Dip the end of the yarn in the melted crayon (wax).

3. Allow it to sit a couple of minutes on a paper towel until hardened.

Tie a knot in the other end. Then have the children string the yarn through the cereal. When complete, give to Mother for Mother's Day.

I Love Mother Book

Have children make books containing what they like about their mothers. Write the words for the small children and have them draw pictures on the pages. Let the older children write and illustrate their books. Make decorative covers for the books by covering poster board with wrapping paper. Punch holes through the covers and pages and bind the books together with ribbon or yarn.

Coupon Book

Have the children make coupon books of chores they would like to do for their mothers.

Play Time

Play house and all can have a turn pretending to be the mother—both boys and girls. Or the boys could pretend to be the father and the girls pretend to be the mother.

Physical Exercise—Game

Play the game Mother, May I? For this outdoor game, the "mother" stands at one end of the yard and the children at the other end. The object of the game is to reach Mother by following Mother's instructions only after having said, "Mother, may I?" The child who is "Mother" starts by calling out a child's name and says, for example, "You may take three giant steps" or "You may take three somersaults." The child responds by saying, "Mother, may I?" The "Mother" either says "Yes, you may," or "No, you may not." If the child proceeds in following the directive before saying, "Mother, may I?," he or she must return to the starting position. The first child to reach the "mother," based on the instructions given, wins and becomes the next "mother."

Story Time

Read stories from children's magazines about mothers or Mother's Day (try *Highlights for Children* and *Sesame Street* magazine).

Father's Day

Happy Father's Day Ties

Items needed: poster board, stamps, stickers, colored markers, large stapler, and ½"-wide elastic.

Cut a necktie out of poster board. Write "Dad" at the top and "Happy Father's Day" at the bottom. Let the children color and decorate with stamps, stickers, and colored markers. Staple both ends of a 12" piece of elastic (about ½" wide) to the top of the necktie. Dad puts the tie on by putting the elastic around his neck.

Bookmarks

Items needed: poster board, stickers, stamps, glue, photo of each child, clear contact paper, pinking shears, hole punch, scissors, and yarn or ribbon.

Cut out bookmarks from poster board. Have the children color the bookmarks and decorate with stickers or stamps. Write "Happy Father's Day" on the bookmarks. If desired, glue a photo of the child to the bookmark. Cover with clear contact paper. Trim with pinking shears. Punch a hole at the top. For the tassel, cut two pieces of yarn (or ribbon) 6" long. Fold the two pieces of yarn so that there are four single strands on one end and two loops on the other. Push the double loop through the hole in the bookmark and pull the other ends through the double loop.

Play Time

Play house and all can have a turn pretending to be the father—

both boys and girls. Or the boys could pretend to be the father and the girls pretend to be the mother.

Physical Exercise

Act out activities the children like to do with Father such as hiking, fishing, basketball, baseball, miniature golf, swimming, skating, etc.

Story Time

Read stories from children's magazines about fathers or Father's Day (try *Highlights for Children* and *Sesame Street* magazine).

Independence Day

Flag

Explain to the children the meaning and significance of the flag. Have the children color pictures of the flag.

Physical Fitness/Music

March to patriotic music. Use rhythm instruments (can be purchased, homemade, or checked out from your local toy library).

Story Time

Read books about our country from your local library. We suggest *It's the Fourth of July* by Stan Hoig, *Doodle Dandy* by Lynda Graham-Barber, and *Fourth of July* by Lynda Sorensen.

Decorations

Decorate your facility with red, white, and blue decorations, (such as flags, bells, fireworks).

Puzzle

Have the children put together a puzzle of the United States.

Halloween

Jack-O-Lantern Piñatas

Items needed: about three 6″ balloons, newspaper, flour/water mixture, orange paint, black paint, clear mailing tape, and thick string or yarn.

Provide each child with the flour/water mixture, a blown-up balloon, and some strips of newspaper (approximately 3″ x 1″). The flour/water mixture should be the consistency of a gooey paste. Have the children dunk their newspaper pieces in the paste and stick on the balloon. Continue until the balloon is well covered. Young children may need some assistance. Put the children's names on the covered balloons and let them dry for two days. When the balloons are dry, have the children paint the piñatas orange. Let dry for another one or two days. After the orange paint has thoroughly dried, have the children paint faces on the piñatas with black paint. Let dry. Later, pop the balloons inside, make a hole at the top and fill with toys and candy. To hang the piñata, punch a hole near the top using a sharp knife, and thread the string or yarn through the hole you've punched and out the top hole (for filling with prizes). Tie in a knot. Cover the hole at the top with clear mailing tape. One at a time, tie the piñatas to a tree or swing set in your yard. As one of the activities of your Halloween party, have each child (blindfolded) attempt to hit his or her piñata with a bat. Each child can keep the contents of his or her own piñata.

Witch Puppet

Refer to pages 169 and 170 for Witch Puppet pattern and instructions.

Black Spider

Refer to page 171 for Black Spider pattern and instructions.

Dancing Jack-O'-Lantern

Refer to page 171 for Dancing Jack-O'-Lantern pattern and instructions.

Bouncy Tail Black Cat

Refer to pages 172 and 173 for Bouncy Tail Black Cat pattern and instructions.

Flying Ghouls

Items needed: construction paper, hole punch, string or yarn, and tape.

Have children make black cats, bats, witches, and ghosts out of construction paper. Punch a hole at the top and tie a string or yarn to the top. Tape each one by the string to a spoke of your ceiling fan (if you have one). Turn the fan on low and watch the witches, bats, ghosts, and black cats fly around. Let the children bring them home at the end of the day.

Decorations

Decorate your day-care facility for Halloween. A talking or screaming doormat is fun to have when the children come to your door each morning.

Story Time

Read Halloween books from your local library for example, *My First Halloween Book* by Colleen L. Reece, *Halloween* by D. J. Herda, and *We Celebrate Halloween* by Bobbie Kalman.

Music

Obtain a tape of eerie music and sounds. Have the children creep around to the music.

Pumpkin Patch

Take a field trip to a pumpkin patch and let each child pick out his/her own pumpkin.

Ghosts

Items needed: Tootsie Pops, string or yarn, black marker, and white facial tissue.

Have children cover their lollipops with a facial tissue. Tie a string around the lollipop at the top of the stick. Let children draw a face with black marker. They can take their ghosts home and eat them later.

Halloween Costume Party

Have the children come in costume on Halloween. Take a group picture and make a copy for every parent. Have a Halloween carnival (i.e., bean bag toss/ring toss /fish pond with candy for prizes, spook alley, bobbing for apples) or have a jack-o'-lantern piñata party.

Thanksgiving

Turkeys

Items needed: Styrofoam balls (small and medium size), feathers, craft eyes, small piece of red felt, toothpicks, and Play-Doh.

With a toothpick attach the two Styrofoam balls to each other, one for the body, the other for the head. Stick feathers into the body (the larger Styrofoam ball). Glue eyes to the head and cut a small triangular piece of red felt to put under the turkey's chin. Insert toothpicks for legs. Insert small balls of Play-Doh into the legs for feet.

Indian Headband

Items needed: construction paper, stapler or glue.

From construction paper, cut out long slender strips of paper and measure to fit around each child's head. Cut out various colors of feathers from construction paper and staple or glue to the long strip to make an Indian headband. Once decorated, connect the headband by stapling together both ends of the long strip.

Pilgrim Girl and Boy

Refer to pages 174 and 175 for pictures of a Pilgrim girl and boy. Have the children color these pictures.

Mr. Curly Tail Turkey

Refer to page 176 for Mr. Curly Tail Turkey pattern and instructions.

Finger-Paint Turkey

Items needed: paintbrushes, finger paints, and white paper.

Using a paintbrush and finger paints, paint each child's hand using a different color for each finger. Press onto white paper. Have each child draw on the turkey's head and feet.

Story Time

Read books about Thanksgiving from your local library such as *Molly's Pilgrim* by Barbara Cohen, *Garfield's Thanksgiving* by Jim Davis, and *Thanksgiving* by Laura Alden.

Music

Sing Thanksgiving songs, such as "Mr. Gobble Gobble Turkey, "The Turkey Trot" and "Five Fat Turkeys," all by Bev Green from Kapers for Kids.

Thankfulness

Make a list of all the things each child is thankful for and let each child take his or her list home.

Decorations

Decorate your day-care facility for Thanksgiving with posters/pictures of turkeys, Pilgrims, Indians, and harvest bounty.

Christmas

Santa's Secret Shop

Send out a flyer ahead of time letting the parents know about this event (refer to page 178). The children need to bring some money on this day. Have the children complete a form listing for whom they would like to buy gifts.

Example:
Grandma __2__ Grandpa __1__ Mom_1__ Dad_1_Sister_2_
Brother _____ Friend (Boy)_____ Friend (Girl) _____ Baby _____

Use these forms as a reference when you go to purchase gifts. Pick up inexpensive items at dollar and discount stores. Set up a store to display the gifts to be sold. Add price tags to the items or group by price. Charge about 50 cents to $2 per item. In the flyer, inform the parents of what the cost of the gifts will be. This activity teaches children about money and mathematics as they shop for items. After all of the children have purchased their items (with your help), wrap them. You may let the older children help with the wrapping. You may want to use wrapping paper the children have made themselves. At the end of the day let the children take the gifts home to give to family members on Christmas.

Decorate

Decorate your day-care center for Christmas. On my front door I have a Santa Claus that says, "Ho, ho, ho, Merry Christmas!" then plays a Christmas tune. The children like this when they come in the morning.

Pine Cone Christmas Trees

Items needed: pine cones (one for each child), green paint, glitter or confetti, and glue.
Have the children paint their pine cones green. Let dry. Let the

children pour dabs of glue on parts of their pine cone and then sprinkle glitter or confetti on them.

Paper Chains

Items needed: colored construction paper (preferably green and red), stapler or glue.

Cut strips of colored construction paper about 4" x 1". Shape into a circle and staple or glue together to make chains for the Christmas tree or to decorate your facility.

Story Time

Read books about Christmas, which may be obtained from your local library. For example, try *The Polar Express* by Chris Van Allsburg, *Christmas Eve on Sesame Street* by Jon Stone, and *The Night Before Christmas* by Clement C. Moore. Read stories about other holidays celebrated around Christmastime by others.

Music

Sing Christmas songs ("Jingle Bells," "I'm Gettin' Nuttin' for Christmas," "Jolly Old St. Nicholas"). Choose one of your favorite holiday songs and change some of the words to bring some personal meaning to you and your day-care kids. Also, for fun, go Christmas caroling to a few of your neighbor friends.

Movie Time

View *Rudolf, the Red-Nosed Reindeer*, *The Grinch Who Stole Christmas*, *Frosty, the Snowman*, or other Christmas favorites.

Snowflakes

Items needed: white paper and scissors.

Teach the children how to make snowflakes by folding and cutting white paper. Decorate the day-care facility with them.

Wrapping Paper

Items needed: white butcher paper and one or more of the

following: stamps, stickers, finger paint, potato stamps, shaped sponges, paint, crayons, or magazines.

Have the children decorate large sheets of butcher paper. The paper can be decorated with stamps, stickers, finger paints, potato stamps, shaped sponges dipped in paint, pictures from magazines, crayon drawings, etc. Let dry. Use as wrapping paper.

Potato Stamp Wrapping Paper

Items needed: potatoes, knife, paint, and butcher paper.

Cut a potato in half. With the potato half, carve out a design (a star, a bell, for example) by removing potato flesh surrounding your design so that the design is raised. Dip in paint and stamp onto a large sheet of butcher paper. Let dry. Use for wrapping paper.

Christmas Cards

Items needed: construction paper or card stock and washable markers.

Cut out cards from construction paper or card stock. Have the children draw designs with the markers. Have the children tell you what to write inside the card.

Red-Nosed Reindeer Surprise Bag

Refer to page 177 for Red-Nosed Reindeer Surprise Bag pattern and instructions.

Tree Ornaments

Items needed: plaster of Paris tree ornaments, paint, paintbrushes, glossy finish, and string.

You can pick up ready-to-paint Christmas tree ornaments made from plaster of Paris at your local craft store. Have the children paint the ornaments. Spray with glossy finish and tie a string through the hole at the top.

Salt Dough Ornaments

Items needed:

- 2 cups flour
- ½ cup salt
- ¾ cup water
- mixing bowl
- rolling pin
- cookie cutters

- toothpick
- aluminum foil
- a cookie sheet
- a paintbrush
- acrylic paints
- string or narrow ribbon

You may choose to let the children help and watch you with the dough process or you may prefer to make the ornaments yourself and let the children paint them. Mix the flour, salt and water in the bowl. Knead the dough on a board until it is soft but not sticky. Roll the dough to about thickness of ½". Cut out the shapes with the cookie cutters. Using the toothpick, make a hole ¼" in diameter near the top of each shape for hanging. Place the dough shapes on a foil-covered cookie sheet. Bake them at 275° F. for about 2 hours. Check them periodically—the ornaments are done when they are completely dry. Remove them from the oven and let them cool. Let the children paint the ornaments with acrylic paints. When the paint is dry, put a piece of string or ribbon through the hole, and tie the ends together to make a loop for hanging.

Santa

Items needed: poster board, stapler, scissors, glue, pink yarn, red felt, craft eyes, and pink pom-pom.

Fold a piece of poster board (or an old postcard) into a cone shape. Staple together and trim any excess. For the face, have the children apply glue to the bottom two-thirds (the wide portion) of the cone and have the children wrap yarn around this part of the cone layer by layer. Make Santa's hat by gluing and covering the top third of the cone with red felt. Trim any excess felt. The hat is glued to pointed end of cone. Face is entire wide end of cone. Top off Santa's hat by gluing a cotton ball to the top of the cone. Glue craft eyes to face. Glue on a pink pom-pom for the nose. Cut out a mouth from red felt and glue to the face. Glue some cotton for a beard and hair on the face.

Birthdays

Decorate your play space when one of your day-care children has a birthday. Have all the children help put up the decorations and make cards for the birthday boy or girl. Have a party! Make it a special day for the child and a fun day for everyone.

6

Taxes and Bookkeeping

Tax laws change, so the information in this chapter is subject to change. You can set up your own bookkeeping system by keeping journals of income and expenses, or you can purchase a book-keeping system specially developed for day care providers. I highly recommend *The Day Care Provider's Easy Bookkeeping System* by Michele Barros. I have found this system very useful in organizing my day-care records. This booklet can be purchased annually (refer to page 130 for ordering information). This booklet provides record-keeping forms, current tax rules, and other helpful information. Other sources are also listed on pages 127, 128, 129, and 131.

Records to Keep

Monthly Expenses

Your monthly expense record should include items such as food, toys, day-care supplies, household supplies, gifts, parties, advertising expense, day-care repairs, magazine subscriptions, craft supplies, workshops, liability insurance premiums, piano rental, video rental, etc. The more you have to deduct, the less taxes you will have to pay at the end of the year. Keep all of your receipts in your day-care filing cabinet. Typically, in this business, you will not incur a significant tax liability because of the number of deductible expenses.

Home and Utility Expenses

Keep a record of the monthly expenses for your home and utilities, such as rent or mortgage interest, property taxes, home or rental insurance, household maintenance and repairs, natural gas, oil, wood, electric, water, garbage, cable TV, and homeowner association dues.

Mileage Record Form

Keep a record of trip mileage when transporting your day-care children, shopping for your day-care supplies, your attendance at related workshops, and so on. This mileage can be deducted as an expense. In 1995, you were allowed to deduct 30 cents a mile for business auto expense. You will need to obtain the current mileage rate.

Equipment Purchased to Be Depreciated

Keep a record of equipment purchased such as: swing set, TV, VCR, camera, refrigerator, play house, computer, and kitchen table. Depending on the amount of usage for your day care, these items may be deducted as a one-time expense or depreciated over a number of years.

Home Improvements for Day Care

Record expenses associated with home improvements for your day-care facility.

Food Program Reimbursements

Monthly you will receive a check reimbursing you for the previous month's food expense. Keep the check stubs in a file in your filing cabinet. This money is considered income (along with day-care earnings) and must be claimed on your taxes at year-end. Your food purchases are claimed as expenses and your food reimbursements as income.

Attendance and Income

Keep accurate records of attendance and income. File your weekly attendance sheets (refer to sample in page 140) in your filing cabinet. The attendance information should be transferred monthly to an income/expense journal or record. This allows you to have two copies of all of your attendance records to help protect against loss or damage. Issue receipts to parents when they pay. Keep the carbon copy as an additional record. Place your old receipt books with the carbons in a basket, file, or storage box labeled "day-care income receipts."

Year-End Tally Sheet

A year-end tally sheet summarizes your income and expenses for the year. This information will serve as a good reference as you prepare your Schedule C and other tax forms.

Tax Forms

Current Tax Forms You May Need (Subject to Change)

Schedule C (Business Profit or Loss), 8829 (Expenses for Business Use of Your Home), W-10 (Dependent Care Provider's Information—one for each parent and a copy for yourself), SS-4 (Application for Employer ID Number), and W-4 (Withholding Allowances—if hiring employees).

Consult a tax professional familiar with applicable tax laws, read current tax publications, or call the IRS at 1-800-442-1040.

Preparing Your Taxes

You may want to use a tax professional to help you with your taxes—at least the first year. Choose one who is experienced with the application of tax law in relation to a day-care business. If you choose a competent tax professional, you can use the first year's forms as a model in helping you to prepare and file your own taxes thereafter. Keep abreast of new tax laws. One way to do this is by attending workshops on day-care taxes. In addition, other good sources of new tax-law information include tax instruction booklets, the IRS, and instructions provided with various day-care accounting systems (for example, *Day Care Provider's Easy Bookkeeping System*).

Keeping Organized

I like to keep a basket where I can deposit receipts when I come home from shopping. Then, when I get time, I write the information from the receipts into my bookkeeping system and file the receipts in a 9″ x 12″ manila envelope located in my day-care filing cabinet. Your annual bookkeeping system booklets may also be filed.

7

Food

Food Program and Meal Planning

Much of your time as a day-care provider will be spent in meal planning, food purchasing, food preparation, serving food, and cleaning up after eating. It is necessary to find ways to make these tasks easier, less time consuming, more economical, more nutritious, and more fun.

I recommend getting on the USDA Child and Adult Care Food Program. If you plan to provide meals and snacks for your day-care children, this program will reimburse you for the cost of designated meals and snacks. In return, you must follow the program's guidelines for well-balanced meals and nutritious snacks. This requires monthly planning and the preparation and submittal of program forms/reports. Menu plans must be approved by the CACFP representative (refer to page 138 for a sample menu plan). Attendance sheets must be completed which indicate the meals and snacks that may be claimed for reimbursement. Attendance sheets and menu plans should be kept on file.

Periodic visits (about three a year depending on the program) are made to your home by a CACFP representative to observe meal and snack time. These visits are usually announced, but may also be unannounced depending on the program. Proper proportions of each food item and a well-balanced meal should be served (such as meat, two fruits or vegetables, bread, and milk). Another requirement of the food program is attendance at one of the program's nutrition workshops each year. I have been on the food program in two different states. Each program was sponsored by a different organization, but both were part of the USDA Child and Adult Care Food Program. The paperwork and rules vary somewhat, but the overall objective is the same: to feed our children nutritious food and keep them healthy. For the phone number of your local USDA CACFP sponsoring organizations, direct an inquiry to your local licensing office or your local Child Care Resource and Referral office.

After your menu plan is developed, you may want to provide a copy to interested parents. Refer to the menu plan as you prepare your shopping list. The following tips may help you save money on your day-care food purchases: (1) stock up on items that are on sale at the grocery store; (2) use coupons on items you intend to buy; (3) shop at club membership stores where you can buy in bulk; and (4) shop at "pack your own" grocery stores which tend to have lower prices.

I recommend buying large cans of natural applesauce. This applesauce can be fed to babies as well as the older children. In feeding babies, the applesauce can also be mixed with rice cereal. In feeding both children and babies, one large can of applesauce may last about a week. You can also purchase other fruit in large cans. If you have fruit trees, pick your own fruit to serve the children.

Crackers purchased in bulk represent an economical as well as nutritious snack. Besides picking up economical and nutritious foods, purchase a few snacks that are just for fun, such as drinks in cute bottles (like Squeezit), animal cookies, Popsicles, squeeze cheese, beef jerky, etc. Upon returning from shopping, deposit receipts from all of your day-care food purchases in your receipt basket. When you have time, record them in your bookkeeping system and save them in your filing cabinet. You may wish to put all of your receipts in an envelope labeled "food" or in with the other receipts labeled by the month or year.

Food Preparation

Choose foods that are easy and quick to prepare or that can be made up ahead of time. Quick and easy food items include:

- microwavable frozen fish sticks
- chicken nuggets
- frozen little hamburgers
- hot dogs
- frozen corn dogs
- canned spaghetti
- sandwiches
- soup
- frozen waffles
- canned vegetables
- canned fruit
- ham
- bread/rolls
- fresh fruit/vegetables
- frozen burritos
- frozen tacos
- frozen taquitos
- frozen pizza
- precut and peeled carrots
- raisins
- carob-coated raisins
- crackers
- beef jerky
- bread sticks
- muffin mixes

When choosing these foods, be sure to follow the guidelines in the CACFP food program. Only certain brands of frozen food may be acceptable. Some foods may need to be homemade or have additional vegetables, cheese, or meat added to the item in order to meet the program's requirements.

Drinks

Children are often thirsty and asking for a drink. Prepare drinks ahead of time in cups labeled with each child's name. You can write on the cups with permanent marker or each child can have their own color. Avoid spills by using cups with lids. Keep the cups in the refrigerator door or on a shelf of the refrigerator in a large container. Keep water in the cups so that cold water is always available to the children. Continue to reuse the cups for other drinks (milk, juice) during the day.

Dishes

Day-care activities don't allow much time for washing dishes, and yet having dirty dishes cluttering up your sink and counter space will not leave your clientele with a good impression. An option for minimizing the use of dishes is to use paper plates and lunch trays. Lunch trays have compartments for separating food which children seem to enjoy. The trays can easily be sprayed off and washed, or placed directly in the dishwasher after use. I tend to use paper plates for snacks and the trays for meals. As much as possible, dish-washing should be limited to trays and silverware. Drink cups can be placed in the dishwasher (or hand washed) at the end of the day.

Serving Food

I provide each child with the same foods and encourage them to eat or (at least taste) everything. For the most part, I haven't had trouble getting children to eat. Most children see other children enjoying their food and decide to eat themselves. I tell the children that after they eat their lunch they can have dessert. There's nothing wrong with dessert if it comes after a balanced meal.

It is important that children get the vitamins they need from their diet. I had a thirteen-month-old girl in my day care who didn't eat well. For her bottle, her mother brought Gatorade. Since the child would not eat solid food or baby food, I felt that she was not getting the nutrition she needed. She cried a lot and had difficulty taking naps. I recommended that the child go back on formula. Concerns about eating habits should be taken up with the parents. The parents may decide to consult their physician.

If you have babies in your day care, you may need high chairs to facilitate spoon-feeding them.

Cleaning Up

Try to clean up immediately after each meal or snack so messes don't pile up. After lunch, send the children outside or to another room while you clean up. If outside, you can watch them out the window while you tidy up. It only takes a few minutes without interruptions.

Nutrition

Keep the meals and snacks nutritious. Serve well-balanced meals. Try to stay away from too much chocolate or sugar, especially before meals. On one occasion, a little girl brought chocolate bars to share with everyone on her birthday. I let her hand the candy out to the other children as a morning snack. The candy ruined everyone's lunch and the children were overly active all day and didn't sleep at nap time. I never repeated that mistake.

Suggestions for healthy snacks include: carrot sticks, celery sticks with cheese spread or peanut butter, fresh cut-up apples or other fresh fruit, Popsicles filled with unsweetened 100 percent fruit juice (make yourself), beef jerky, cheese, bread sticks, muffins, crackers, yogurt, and raisins.

8

Health and Safety

Screening Policy

Although delightful, children can spread germs. You can help prevent the spread of children's diseases by screening each child for visible signs of communicable diseases each day when a child is brought to your day-care home.

Children should be checked before the parent is allowed to leave them. Children who show signs of illness should not be accepted for care (at your discretion). Children who become ill during the day should be isolated from the other children and their parents should be notified to make arrangements for their pickup.

Here are some things to check for before accepting a child in your care: fever over 100 degrees, vomiting or diarrhea, wet and wheezy cough, sore throat, red or yellow eyes, and skin rashes or spots. Children who have these symptoms may return when the symptoms have disappeared or a doctor signs a note that the child has no communicable illness.

The daily screening and exclusion policy (refer to page 135) can have a significant effect on the number of illnesses in a group of children. The application of such a policy is subject to your discretion. A copy of your health screening policy should be given to and signed by the parents.

Even with a screening policy, your children will still get sick. My son was near a child who had chicken pox. We didn't know it until we saw signs of the illness. By then the entire day care had been exposed. I notified the parents that their children had been exposed. The parents were informed of the situation and told that they may want to remove their child from the facility for a time. This was their decision and one in which they may consult with their individual physician.

On a different occasion, I considered caring for three children who had the chicken pox. I was concerned since my own baby girl had not been exposed to the disease yet. My physician advised me to avoid exposure until my child was at least one year old. The experience reaffirmed for me the importance of consulting with a physician. Consequently, I continue to encourage parents to do the same.

Medications

When a parent brings medication for his or her child, authorization for administering the medication should be obtained by having the parent sign a medication authorization form (refer to page 142). The following information should be included on the form: name of child, name of prescription, instructions for administering the medication (that dosage, time to be given), signature of the parent, and date of authorization.

In addition, keep a record of all medications administered (refer to page 143). The record should include: name of child, name of medication, date and time given, and dosage. Only administer medications that are provided by the parent.

Immunizations

Request verification from parents that their children have received the required immunizations before allowing them into your care.

Check with the parents periodically to make sure that their children are up to date on their immunizations.

Emergency Medical Care

It is recommended that you become certified in CPR and first aid. Some states require CPR and first aid certification before issuing a day-care license. Even if your state doesn't require this, it is important for a day-care provider to become trained in CPR. A day-care provider trained in CPR is much better qualified to respond to a medical emergency or life-threatening situation. Local hospitals or fire departments may offer courses in CPR or can refer you to organizations that can provide this type of training.

In the case of an emergency or serious injury, you should immediately notify the child's parent or guardian. Keep a first aid kit that contains (at a minimum) the following items: adhesive bandages, antiseptic solution, sterile bandages, scissors, medical tape, cotton swabs, and syrup of ipecac. Emergency telephone numbers should be conspicuously posted on or beside one or more of your telephones. These phone numbers should include: police, fire, poison control, and the facility's telephone number and address.

Fire Safety

Smoke detectors should be installed in all sleeping areas and hallways. Smoke detector batteries should be tested monthly. Fire extinguishers should be in or near the kitchen and the areas used by children. An evacuation plan should be posted and fire drills should be held once a month. There should be at least two unobstructed, usable exits available to the children. Infants and young children should not be cared for below or above the facility's ground level unless, at that level, there is an exit directly to the outside.

Childproof Your Home

Here are some precautions you can take to childproof your home:

- Place security caps on all electrical outlets.

- Place childproof locks on all cabinets containing dangerous or harmful items.
- Store medicines, makeup, and dangerous chemicals out of reach of children.
- Keep firearms locked up.
- Cover stove knobs with childproof knob covers (available in local discount stores).
- Cover garbage cans and diaper pails.
- Do not allow children to play with rocks or sticks.
- Fences should have no rusty sharp points facing inward.
- There should be no nails left around the yard where children are present.
- Do not have furniture with sharp corners where the children play.
- Keep cords from window coverings up high.
- Fence off any stairways in your home.
- Children should not be allowed to play with ropes or on rope swings.
- Poisonous plants should be inaccessible to children.
- Irrigation ditches, abandoned mines, and wells should be inaccessible to children.
- Fans should be permanently mounted and placed out of the reach of children.
- All fireplaces should be screened.
- Unvented or open-flame heaters and electric portable heaters should not be used.
- Gas lines should be inspected annually.
- Electrical cords should not be within reach of children.
- Place decals on sliding glass doors to prevent children from running through the glass.

Diapering

1. Have a set diaper-changing area away from food preparation and eating areas.
2. Wear rubber gloves when diapering and wash hands afterward.

3. Sanitize the diaper changing pad with bleach solution after each diaper change (one part bleach, nine parts water).
4. Store soiled diapers in a tight container away from the children.

Other Helpful Health and Sanitary Hints

1. Open windows daily to bring in fresh air. Even during the winter months, bring in some fresh air for at least short periods of time. Have children play outside whenever possible. Fresh air is good for children. It allows the body to adapt to changes in air temperature. Keep the room temperature in your home at a comfortable level. A home that is too hot and dry during the winter months is unhealthy for children, parching the nose and throat and lowering resistance to germs.
2. Keep all toys, furniture, and equipment clean and sanitized with bleach/water solution.
3. Have crib sheets washed often and have each child use his or her own sheet.
4. Insect control should include screening of all direct openings to the outside. Doors which open to the outside should not be left open without insect control.
5. Toilet bowls, sinks, and floors should be scrubbed with a disinfectant cleaning solution as needed.
6. Organic waste should be disposed of immediately in a sanitary manner and stored in tightly covered containers lined with plastic bags and secured with tight-fitting covers.
7. Tightly covered outdoor containers for garbage and trash should be available to accommodate all waste products from the facility.

Personal Hygiene and Cleanliness

Good personal hygiene can help prevent the spread of germs in your day-care facility. Hands should be washed with soap and warm water in connection with food handling; use of toilet; diaper changing; and after nose wipe, sneeze catch, or cough cover. Items that can be used in hand washing include:

- antibacterial liquid soap (you can purchase liquid soaps in containers that look like crocodiles or Disney characters, which help to make washing more fun for the children)
- paper towels (cloth towels collect germs)
- child-size stepping stool (to be used in helping the children reach the sink.

Prepare a preschool lesson on personal hygiene (refer to chapter 4 for a unit of instruction on "Good Health Habits").

9

Miscellaneous Concerns

Your Relationship With Parents

Hopefully you will have a good relationship with all of the parents of the children in your care. Many of the parents that I have worked for became good friends. I enjoyed seeing and chatting with them each day. They appreciated the things I did for their children.

At times, parents will offer suggestions. A parent may suggest that you don't feed their child a specific food or recommend that their child take an earlier nap. Welcome their input. As much as possible, attempt to comply with their requests.

You may have to confront a parent with financial concerns. A parent may be behind on his or her payments. This represents a challenging situation, but you must keep in mind that you have a business to run, and as with any other business, you must be paid. You must enforce your contract and charge late fees when necessary. Not being paid can result in negative feelings toward the parent which may affect your attitude and care of his or her children. If a parent does not comply with the conditions of the contract, you may have to drop that child from your care. With the great demand for good child-care providers, you should be able to fill the opening.

Don't be afraid to take a vacation as necessary. I knew a day care provider who was reluctant to take time off after having a baby because she was apprehensive over losing her clientele. If the parents are happy with you, they will use your substitute provider or one of their own, and bring their children back to you.

Involving Parents: Communication and the Well-Being of the Child

The well-being of the child should be the focus of both the parent and the day-care provider. Sometimes I wonder why we, as home day-care providers, don't have more structured means of communicating with the parents. In school, they have parent-teacher conferences and report cards. It is difficult to find the time to have a meaningful dialogue with the parents. In the morning, parents are rushing to get to work on time and in the evening parents are anxious to get home to prepare dinner, relax, and so on. Under such circumstances, important information is not conveyed or discussed. The items for discussion may include the following:

- Is this child eating well enough?
- Should this baby go back on formula?
- In helping the child develop, can the parent refrain from "giving in" to the child's tantrums?
- Does the parent know how well this child is progressing intellectually?

Introduce the parents to the practice of regular parent-provider conferences. Emphasize the benefits to the children of this form of collaboration. Attempt to accommodate the parent's schedule as much as possible. Remember—one or two parent-provider conferences is better than no discussion at all. At the parent-provider conference solicit input; share administrative concerns (such as late pickup, late payments); and most importantly, discuss the activity and progress of the child (his or her mental, emotional, social, and physical development).

Video

Once a year I like to have a movie day for the benefit of the children and their parents. With a camcorder, I make a video of a typical day at my day care. Then I make a copy for each of the parents. This allows the parents to see what their children do all day and is a great memento for years to come.

Scrapbook

A great way to use the photos you take of the children is to make a day-care scrapbook. The album cover can be decorated with fabric and figures/characters associated with your day care. I cover my scrapbook with "Care Bears" which represents the theme of my day care. In addition to photographs, you may want to include in your scrapbook your license certificate, children's artwork, notes/letters written by the children, etc. Periodically, this scrapbook can be set out for the parents to view. Also, when you are meeting with prospective clients, you may want to share with them your scrapbook so that they can get a better idea of the services you provide.

Party

A day-care party can be an effective approach to helping your clients (both parents and children) get better acquainted with one another. The birthday of one of your own children may provide an opportunity to invite all of your day-care children and their parents to a party. It is best to schedule the event at a time when most can attend (on Saturday perhaps).

Infant Care

Depending upon the state, a day-care child is classified as an infant if he or she is either under the age of two or under the age of one. Infants require love and attention. It is heartbreaking to observe too many babies in a day-care facility whose needs are not being met. Create a sense of security for the infant in responding quickly to his or her needs.

There will be times when babies are more irritable than usual. If you have an infant who cries excessively, try to identify the problem (allergy, colic, rash, teething). Discuss your concerns with the parents. Excessive crying is not good for you or the baby.

A six-month-old baby enrolled in my day care home. Soon after, I was told by a friend that she knew a lady who had watched the baby previously and after two weeks of the baby crying so much, she quit. As I began caring for this child, I concluded two possible reasons for the baby's excessive crying: (1) infants need to develop a sense of security and trust in their surroundings and in their caregiver, and this baby had not done that yet; and (2) infants require plenty of sleep and if they are getting too much excitement and attention, they will cry.

The first week or two will be a period of adjustment for you and the new infant in your care. The baby will develop a sense of security as you care for his or her needs during this time. Don't be discouraged and give up too soon.

Babies cry when they are hungry, sick or in pain, tired or bored, feeling insecure, or when they've had too much excitement and attention. The average six-month-old baby needs a one- to three-hour nap every morning and every afternoon. Therefore, a crying six-month-old whose other needs are met (food, diaper change) is probably crying because he or she needs a nap. Many caregivers respond to this in the wrong way—by giving the tired child more excitement and attention (holding and walking the floor with the baby, leaving the baby up and around all the noise of the day-care facility, bouncing the baby, and so forth). This just makes the baby cry more.

Here is a method for putting a tired, overstressed baby to bed:

1. Be sure the baby's other needs (besides sleep) are met.
2. Put the baby to bed in a crib or playpen in a room alone away from noise, give the baby a pacifier, blanket, or whatever baby usually takes to bed, leave the room, and close the door. This approach allows the caregiver as well as the baby a break. It is not good for a caregiver to listen to too much crying which can gradually make the caregiver feel frustrated inside and can lead to negative actions on the caregiver's part (becoming cross with the children, shouting, or

even leading to physically harming children).

3. Let the baby cry and get out his or her frustrations for up to five minutes. No longer than five minutes is necessary.

4. Go in the room after five minutes. Do not get the baby up. Soothe the baby (pat on the back, talking calmly). Put the pacifier in the baby's mouth if the baby will take it. If not, hold a bottle in the baby's mouth until the baby is asleep or almost asleep. Leave the room.

As the baby gets more comfortable with you and his or her new surroundings, the need to let the baby cry will diminish and the baby will go right to sleep when put to bed most of the time.

Here are some tips for caring for infants:

1. Talk to and hold children two years of age and younger frequently throughout the day.

2. Respond promptly to the infant's distress signals and need for comfort.

3. Infants should spend no more than one hour of consecutive time during waking hours confined in a crib, playpen, high chair, or other confining structure.

4. Each infant should be allowed to maintain an individual pattern of sleeping, waking, and eating, unless instructed by the parent or guardian to the contrary.

5. Infants who cannot hold their bottles should be held by the provider while being fed. Bottles should never be propped. (However, if you find it necessary to prop a bottle, be sure that you are watching the baby so that the baby doesn't choke on it).

6. Plastic bottle liners should not be reused. Used bottles should be promptly removed from cribs or beds, emptied, and cleaned.

7. Only water should be used in bedtime or nap-time bottles.

8. Babies should not be fed cereal by bottle.

9. Each infant's or child's diaper should be checked frequently.

10. You should consult with the parent or guardian about toilet training. You should never force toilet training on a child. I believe the parents are responsible for toilet training and

that the role of the day-care provider is to reinforce the instruction and directives of the parents.

11. High chairs, cribs, and other baby equipment should be in safe working order. Crib bars should be spaced no more than 2³/₈" apart. I recommend a good bumper pad for cribs with bars. Without a bumper pad, infants can get their limbs caught between the bars. I have seen circulation cut off and extreme soreness result.

12. Each crib should have clean bedding, including sheets and a blanket.

Night Care

If you choose to provide night care, the following points should be considered:

1. Each infant needs a crib and each child needs a bed or cot.
2. Bathe and shower children only with written permission of parent or guardian.
3. Sanitize bath or shower between uses.
4. You should remain awake until all children are asleep.
5. You may sleep if you are within hearing distance of the children in your care. Do not share the same bed with a child in your care.

Special Needs Children

You may decide to accept children with special needs (such as handicapped, hearing impaired, diabetic) in your facility. If you do, you should first receive instructions from the child's parents about anything special that you need to do for their child. Make accommodations as necessary. As possible, integrate the special needs child into the daily activities of the day-care home.

Transportation of Children

If you plan to provide transportation at any time for the children, here are some guidelines you should follow:

1. Obtain written authorization from the child's parent or

guardian prior to transporting enrolled children.

2. Vehicle should be maintained in a mechanically safe condition.
3. You need to hold a current state driver's license.
4. Do not let children ride in the back of a pickup truck.
5. Each child should have a seatbelt.
6. Children four years of age or younger and weighing forty pounds or less should be in a child safety seat.
7. Your vehicle must be equipped with air conditioning and heating.
8. A first aid kit should be in your vehicle.
9. Immediately report any traffic accident involving children being transported by you.
10. Keep the doors locked when the vehicle is in motion.
11. Never leave children unattended in a vehicle.
12. Do not allow children to open or close the vehicle doors.

Field Trip Requirements:

13. Obtain written permission from the parent or guardian before the field trip.
14. Take a copy of the emergency information for each child with you on the field trip.
15. Each child should have on his or her person, in plain view, the provider's name, address, and telephone number. The child's first and last name should be placed inconspicuously on his or her person.

Burnout

Many day care providers experience "burnout" from time to time. In Webster's *New World Dictionary, burnout* is defined as "the state of emotional exhaustion caused by the stresses of one's work or responsibilities." Certainly in the day-care business we can experience emotional exhaustion from the work that we do. What can you do about it?

1. Network with other providers or at-home moms. I had a friend in my neighborhood who also had a home day care. It

helped to get together with her so that I had some adult companionship during the day. Occasionally we would visit one another. We also got together for outings at the park and day-care parties.

2. Be creative and have fun. Plan some fun activities (like parties) with the children. Having something to look forward to that will represent a break in the routine can be quite satisfying.

3. Go on vacation! You need a vacation from time to time just like others who work. You will find that you can make it through a time of burnout if you know you have a vacation coming up soon. Be prepared to treat yourself to a vacation as necessary. It helps to have a backup so that you are not placed in the position of having to ask your clients to find their own substitutes.

4. Seek out additional training opportunities or books on family day care. Learn about approaches and techniques that will make your job easier and more rewarding.

5. Cut back. Maybe you are trying to do too much. Perhaps a reduction in hours or children will help the situation to become more manageable. In some cases, dropping a child who represents a significant challenge may be the answer. Rather than a full-time day care, you may want to consider a part-time preschool. You may know another provider who would like to work alternating weeks. If the parents agree to this arrangement, you can have every other week off. For some, day care is more feasible as a temporary business (one or two years). Or you may want to consider taking a break from day care with the option of returning to it later.

6. Take care of yourself. Try to find some time just for you—in rest and relaxation or in pursuing one of your interests or hobbies.

Reporting Suspected Child Abuse

During your experience as a child care provider you may see children who have been harmed, sexually molested, or neglected by their parents or guardian. When an abused or neglected child is enrolled in your child care, you may literally save the child's life by reporting suspected abuse to child protective services.

You may be reluctant to report suspected child abuse. However, it is a law that suspected child abuse should be reported. The requirements vary from state to state. Each child care provider needs to check with the state in which their facility is located to determine the reporting requirements for that state. These reporting requirements should be incorporated into the policies and procedures for the day-care program.

You are not required to have proof that abuse has occurred prior to making the report, only that it is suspected. Most state laws expect child abuse to be reported as soon as it is suspected. Failure to do so may result in civil or criminal penalties.

All states provide immunity from liability to reporters of suspected child abuse when the report is made in "good faith" and is found to be unsubstantiated. It is important that the child care provider document the incident, including the basis for the suspicion. A sample reporting form is included on page 144 that satisfies most of the reporting requirements. A copy of this form should be kept in the facility's day-care filing cabinet.

Each state has an agency designated to be the central reporting authority for child abuse within that state. The staff of these agencies should be available to provide additional information to the child-care provider and may be available to provide training.

Some possible indicators of neglect are poor personal hygiene, ravenous hunger, no immunizations or other medical and dental care, and severe cases of diaper rash.

Some possible indicators of physical abuse are:

1. Bruises—bruises on the abdomen or back may be present (areas of the body not usually bruised in normal childhood activities). Bruises may be different colors showing various stages of healing. There may be bruises on the upper arms where the abuser tightly gripped the child and violently shook him or her. There may be bruise-like coloration around the eyes called "raccoon eyes" indicating shaking of

around the eyes called "raccoon eyes" indicating shaking of the infant. Internally, there may be bleeding around the brain.

2. Burns—cigarette burns are strong indicators of abuse. Also, rope burns around ankles, wrists, or neck. Wet burns from hot water, and dry burns from irons or stove burners are possible signs of abuse.

3. Fractures—multiple fractures in various stages of healing are likely to be evidence of physical abuse. Swollen or tender limbs, spiral fractures, rib fractures, or bones that have been injured are all possible signs of child abuse.

4. Lacerations and abrasions—when found on the soft tissue areas of the abdomen, the back, on the backs of arms and legs, or external genitalia lacerations and abrasions strongly suggest physical abuse, as do human bite marks, especially if recurrent and adult size.

Some possible indicators of sexual abuse are:

1. age inappropriate understanding of sex
2. reluctance to be left alone with a particular person
3. persistent and inappropriate sex play with peers or toys
4. wearing lots of clothing, especially to bed
5. drawings with genitals
6. fear of touch
7. abuse of animals
8. masturbation in public
9. nightmares or night terrors
10. apprehension when subject of sex, genitals, or sexual abuse is brought up

Finding Substitute Caregivers

Finding substitute caregivers is a necessary step in beginning your day-care operation. Some hesitate to get into day care because they believe the demands of the business will not allow them to run errands, take vacations, schedule appointments, and so on. However, prearranged substitutes can free up time during the day for such activities.

It is good to know at least two or three individuals who could be available to substitute. Some prefer not to have a full-time day care, but would like to earn a little extra money by substituting. Or other home day-care providers with openings may consider pinch-hitting from time to time. Arrangements can be made for the substitute to come to your home or the children can be cared for in the substitute's home.

Pay the substitute for his or her time (a little more than you would actually make in that amount of time). When sick, arrange for the parents to bring the children to the substitute's home.

The parents will appreciate your effort in finding a substitute for them. Parents always have the option of using your substitute or finding their own. After having a new baby, I took a month off. During that time, two different substitutes cared for the children in the providers' own homes.

Appendix A

Note: In order to use the materials provided in this section, all forms should be enlarged to a size of 8½" x 11".

RESOURCES FOR DAY-CARE PROVIDERS

Day-Care Equipment and Toys

Environments, Inc.
Box 1348
Beaufort, SC 29901-1348
1-800-EI-CHILD

Preschool Programs

Kapers for Kids, Inc.
2325 Endicott St.
Saint Paul, MN 55114
1-800-882-7332

Home Preschool Program
23382 Maero Rd., Unit D
Mission Viejo, CA 92691
714-951-3946

Children's Videos

Some of these videos can be purchased from your local discount department store. Others may be special ordered for you by your local video and music sales and rental store.

Scamper, The Penguin
Celebrity Home Entertainment
by Feature Films for Families
1-800-347-2833

Dot and the Whale
Family Home Entertainment

The Land Before Time
MCA Home Video
Lucas/ Spielberg, Don Bluth

Richard Scarry's Best ABC Video Ever
Random House

Mousercise
Walt Disney

*Dr. Seuss's ABC's and
    Other Stories*
Random House

Barney and Friends
The Lyon's Group

Walt Disney Film Classics
Walt Disney

Disney Sing-A-Longs
Walt Disney

*Richard Scarry's Best Counting
    Video Ever*
Random House

*Richard Scarry's Best Busy
    People Video Ever*
Random House

Sesame Street
Children's Television
Workshop

Charlotte's Web
Paramount

Disney Babies Playtime
Walt Disney Records
This tape contains about 45 minutes of fun action songs for children, including: Itsy Bitsy Spider; Here is the Church; The Wheels on the Bus; Head, Shoulders, Knees and Toes; and more.

Disney Babies Lullaby
Walt Disney Records
This tape contains about 45 minutes of lullabies for children, including: Rockabye Baby; Brahms Lullaby; When You Wish Upon a Star; La La Lu; and more.

Disney's Silly Songs
Walt Disney Records
This tape contains 20 silly songs, including: Boom, Boom, Ain't It Great to be Crazy?, Michael Finnegan, and Baby Bumblebee.

Wee Sing Dinosaurs
Price/Stern/Sloan
This tape contains one hour of musical enternment featuring 50 original, fact-filled songs and poems and a 65-page book with complete lyrics.

Barney's Favorites—Vol. 1
5BK Records

This tape contains some of the songs from the hit television program, including: My Family's Just Right For Me; Clean Up; Sally The Camel; Do Your Ears Hang Low; and more.

Wee Sing for Baby
Price/Stern/Sloan
This tape contains about one hour of music including 65 baby games and lullabies and a 64-page illustrated book with lyrics.

Children's Games

Teddy Bear Bingo	Giant Old Maid
Milton Bradley	Western Publishing Company
Mickey Mouse Yahtzee	The Busy World of Richard Scarry
Milton Bradley	Busiest Shopping Day Ever Game
Giant Fish	Golden
Western Publishing Company	Peanut Butter and Jelly
	Parker Preschool
Connect Four	Candy Land
Milton Bradley	Milton Bradley
Crazy Eights	Barnyard Bingo
Creative Child Games	Fisher-Price

Day-Care Insurance

Insurance Marketing Center (Jefferson General Agent)
14500 Burnhaven Drive, Suite 135
Burnsville, MN 55306-6199
1-612-435-1606/Wats 1-800-245-0023

Adult's and Children's Alliance
2885 Country Drive, Suite 165
Saint Paul, MN 55117-2621
1-800-433-8108

Tax Help

ABC's and 123's Publishing
9619 Windham
Stockton, CA 95209
1-800-233-8220
Call or write to order
the *Day Care Provider's*
Easy Bookkeeping System
by Michele and Barry Barros

Redleaf Press
A Division of Resources for Child Caring
450 N. Syndicate, Suite 5
Saint Paul, MN 55104-4125
To order: 1-800-423-8309
Fax: 1-800-641-0115
Calendar-Keeper (Current year);
The Basic Guide to Family Child Care Record Keeping by Tom Copeland;
(Current year) *Tax Workbook* by Tom Copeland

Professional Organizations

Professional Daycare Providers Association
IMC Inc., 14500 Burnhaven Drive, Suite 135
Burnsville, MN 55306-6199
1-800-245-0023

Child Care Services System
ACA
2885 Country Drive, Suite 165
Saint Paul, MN 55117-2621
1-800-433-8108

Community and Government Resources

CHILD-CARE RESOURCE AND REFERRAL

This agency may assist you in the following ways: client referrals, responding to inquiries, newsletters, training workshops, informative literature, and day-care provider group sessions (meetings in which day-care providers get together to discuss relevant topics).

DAY-CARE PROVIDER'S TOY LENDING LIBRARY

Attempt to locate a toy lending library in your community. You can direct an inquiry to your local licensing agency or Child Care Resource and Referral Agency. The libraries may have the following items or services available: toys for day-care use, books on relevant topics (for example, child development, circle time lessons, child discipline), and equipment for lamination and duplication of materials.

WORKSHOPS AND TRAINING CONFERENCES

Various government agencies may offer workshops and conferences. You may become aware of these through your affiliation with the Food Program, Child Care Resource and Referral Agency, or your State Licensing Office.

USDA CHILD AND ADULT CARE FOOD PROGRAM

This program can provide you with help which may include: financial reimbursements for money spent on food, training workshops, nutrition information, newsletters, and other helpful literature.

STATE LICENSING OFFICE

The licensing office can assist you as follows: provide information relative to home safety requirements, respond to inquiries, conduct training workshops, inspect your home, provide necessary forms, and so on.

CHILD CARE RESOURCE AND REFERRAL
CUSTOMER REFERRAL RESPONSE LETTER

FOLLOWING IS A LIST OF CHILD CARE PROVIDERS AND INFORMATION ABOUT THEM
THAT HAS BEEN MATCHED BY COMPUTER WITH YOUR PARTICULAR CHILD CARE
NEEDS. FEEL FREE TO CONTACT THESE PROVIDERS AND ARRANGE FOR A MUTUALLY
ACCEPTABLE APPOINTMENT.

FACILITY NAME	KIDS ARE FUN DAY CARE		**TELEPHONE**	538-9584
CONTACT PERSON	TINA WEST		**REGISTRATION FEE $**	0.00
NEAREST SCHOOL	BRAVEHART		**WALKING DISTANCE**	2 BLKS
TYPE OF CARE	FAMILY HOME			
TIMES AND SHIFTS	FULL-TIME. PART-TIME. FULL YEAR. FLEX-TIMES. WEEKENDS			
AGES ACCEPTED	BIRTH TO 12 YEARS		**HOURS ACCEPTED**	6 AM TO 6 PM
AGE GROUP	0-23 MONTHS	2-2.9 YEARS	2.9 - 5 YEARS	6 +
COMMON COSTS	75.00/WK	65.00/WK	65.00/WK	2.00/HR
SPECIAL NEEDS	PROVIDES TRANSPORT, HANDICAPPED, SICK CARE, DROP-IN			
ENVIRONMENT	OUT DOOR PLAY AREA. GYM			
CURRICULUM				
CERTIFICATIONS				
COMMENTS	ENVIRONMENT JUST FOR CHILDREN, ARTS & CRAFTS			

FACILITY NAME	COUNTRY TIME DAY CARE		**TELEPHONE**	521-5434
CONTACT PERSON	SUSAN FRY		**REGISTRATION FEE $**	0.00
NEAREST SCHOOL	JEFFERSON		**WALKING DISTANCE**	1 BLK
TYPE OF CARE	FAMILY HOME			
TIMES AND SHIFTS	FULL-TIME. PART-TIME. PART WEEK. FLEX-TIMES. TEMP/EMERG			
AGES ACCEPTED	BIRTH TO 10 YEARS		**HOURS ACCEPTED**	7 AM TO 5 PM
AGE GROUP	0-23 MONTHS	2-2.9 YEARS	2.9 - 5 YEARS	6 +
COMMON COSTS	75.00/WK	65.00/WK	65.00/WK	2.13/HR
SPECIAL NEEDS	HANDICAPPED, SICK CARE. DROP-IN			
ENVIRONMENT	NON SMOKING HOME. OUT DOOR PLAY AREA			
CURRICULUM				
CERTIFICATIONS	ECE TRAINED			
COMMENTS	PLAYROOM, NINTENDO, STORYTIME. MUSIC SING-A-LONG			

Appendix A

LICENSING REPORT

FACILITY NAME Carolyn's Child Care		FACILITY NUMBER 500315204		FACILITY TYPE FDC		
ADDRESS 1113 Pine Tree	TELEPHONE 544-8432	CAPACITY 6	CENSUS 4	DATE 8-5-92		
TYPE OF VISIT: ☐ OFFICE ☐ PRELICENSING	☐ RENEWAL ☐ EVALUATION	☐ COMPLAINT ☐ FOLLOW-UP	☒ MANAGEMENT ☐ OTHER	☐ ANNOUNCED ☒ UNANNOUNCED	TIME VISIT BEGAN	TIME COMPLETED 2:30

DEFICIENCY INFORMATION:	CIVIL PENALTY INFORMATION:

COMMENTS/DEFICIENCIES	RECOMMENDATIONS/CORRECTIONS
Case management visit completed by Evaluator Smith.	
Mrs. Argyle was providing care for four children.	
All in good order.	
Home is clean and well maintained.	

LICENSING EVALUATOR SIGNATURE	TELEPHONE	DATE 8-5-92	I understand my licensing appeal rights.	
NAME OF SUPERVISOR	TELEPHONE	FACILITY REPRESENTATIVE SIGNATURE		DATE

PROVIDER-PARENT AGREEMENT-CONTRACT

I agree to enroll my child, _____, in the
_____ Family Day-Care Home, beginning
on _____. I have received and read the attached Family
Day-Care Policies and agree to comply with all rules and responsibilities stated in them.

(1)   Care will normally begin at _____ o'clock and end at _____
      o'clock on the following days of the week:
      _____

(2)   Care will include the following meals and snacks:
      _____
      _____

(3)   The charge for care of the child is $_____ per _____.
      Overtime charges are $_____ per _____.
      There will be a charge of $_____ if a child is picked up after
      _____ o'clock.

(4)   Payment to the Day-Care Provider will be made in the following
      manner: Cash _____ Check _____ by _____
      (name of person to pay), on _____ (day of the week
      or month).

      Payment is due based on the hours you *agree* to use child care
      whether or not the child actually attends. Vacations arranged by
      advance will be allowed without regular payment to the Day-
      Care Provider.

(5)   Children may be taken from the Day-Care Provider's care only
      by the person signed below, or other friend or relative if
      permission is given by person signed below.

Parent's Signature(s)   _____
                          _____
                          _____
Date Signed   _____

DAY-CARE POLICIES

1. Meals and snacks are provided for the children by the Day-Care Provider.

2. Please bring your own diapers, bottles, pacifiers, and blankets.

3. When the Day-Care Provider is not available during normal day-care hours (e.g., doctor's appointment), the Day-Care Provider will find a substitute who can watch the children during that time. When the Day-Care Provider takes vacation, the Day-Care Provider will assist in finding a substitute for the parents.

4. Items included in the program:
   • morning preschool program including: music, language arts, math and science, stories, arts and crafts, and physical activity
   • outdoor play area: swing set, lawn, and sand box
   • puzzles, work papers, computer learning programs, and coloring in the afternoon for stickers on a chart to receive prizes
   • breakfast if before 7:30 A.M., morning snack, lunch, and afternoon snack
   • nap time from noon to 2:00 P.M.

5. Rate of payment: $2.00/hr—part-time, $60/week—full-time, and $65/week—infants.

6. Bad check policy:
   • first occurrence—charge of $10 for the bad check
   • second occurrence—all future payments must be made in cash.

7. Discipline policy:
   • Rules are established and clearly communicated to the child.
   • If a rule is disobeyed, the child is reminded to obey the rule.
   • Time-out when necessary (2 minutes in the corner).

8. Sample of rules:
   • No hitting or hurting other children.
   • Get along and share toys.
   • Listen during preschool time.
   • Obey the Day-Care Provider.

9. Health screening policy—To help reduce the spread of illness, please do not bring your child if he/she has any of the following symptoms:
   • vomiting or diarrhea
   • cough (wet, wheezy with mucous secretion)
   • throat and neck infection
   • eye redness, discharge, or yellowness
   • skin rashes, spots, eruptions, vermin, etc.
   • opaque and/or bloody discharge from nose and ears
   • temperature over 100 degrees.

Identification and Emergency Information

					DATE RECORD UPDATED

CHILD'S NAME (Last, First, M.I.)			BIRTHDATE	SEX ☐M ☐F
HOME ADDRESS (No., Street, City, State, ZIP)				HOME PHONE
MOTHER'S NAME (or Guardian)	BUSINESS ADDRESS (No., Street, City, State, ZIP)			DAYTIME PHONE
FATHER'S NAME (or Guardian)	BUSINESS ADDRESS (No., Street, City, State, ZIP)			DAYTIME PHONE

IN EMERGENCY (If parent cannot be reached) NOTIFY

NAME (First, Last)	PHONE	RELATIONSHIP
ADDRESS (No., Street, City, State, ZIP)		
NAME (First, Last)	PHONE	RELATIONSHIP
ADDRESS (No., Street, City, State, ZIP)		

IF MEDICAL CARE IS NECESSARY, CALL

DOCTOR'S NAME	PHONE
ADDRESS (No., Street, Suite or Room No., City)	
HOSPITAL OF CHOICE	PHONE

In case of injury or sudden illness, I hereby give authority to the above-named doctor or hospital to render immediate emergency aid as might by required at the time for the child's health and safety.
I understand that I will be responsible for the expense of this service.

PARENT OR GUARDIAN'S SIGNATURE	DATE

MEDICAL INFORMATION

IMMUNIZATIONS	DATES					ALLERGIC TO:
	1	2	3	4	5	
DTP or TD -						MEDICATION(S)
Polio (oral drops) -						
Measles (red or hard) -						FOOD(S)
Mumps -						
Rubella (German) Measles -						OTHER(S)
MR (Measles/Rubella) -						
MMR (Measles/Mumps/Rubella) -						
Tetanus, Haemophilus -						
Influenza, Type B (Hib) -						
Hepatitis B Vaccine (HBV) -						

SPECIAL DIET REQUIREMENTS

OTHER SPECIAL INSTRUCTIONS

CHILD MAY ONLY BE PICKED UP BY (Individuals picking up children must be at least 18 years of age; check ID carefully)

NAME (First, Last)	PHONE	RELATIONSHIP	AGE
NAME (First, Last)	PHONE	RELATIONSHIP	AGE
NAME (First, Last)	PHONE	RELATIONSHIP	AGE

ONLY those named above are authorized to pick up my child.	PARENT OR GUARDIAN'S SIGNATURE	DATE

AFFIDAVIT REGARDING LIABILITY INSURANCE
FOR FAMILY DAY CARE HOME

I/We, the parent(s)/guardian(s) of _____ ,
Child's Name

acknowledge that _____ ,
Licensee's Name

the licensee of _____
Name of Family Day Care Home

has informed me/us that this facility does not carry liability insurance or a bond in
accordance with standards established by Family Day Care statute.

SIGNATURE OF PARENT(S)/ LEGAL GUARDIAN(S)	DATE

MENU PLAN

PROVIDER'S NAME: Carolyn Argyle   WEEKLY PLAN #1   1992

REVIEWED BY: MD

	MONDAY	TUESDAY	WEDNESDAY	THURSDAY	FRIDAY	SATURDAY	SUNDAY
BREAKFAST							
Milk	MILK	MILK	MILK	MILK	MILK	MILK	MILK
Fruit, veg or Juice	banana	orange j.	raisins	apple j.	apple	strawberries	apple
Bread or Alternate	Cheerios	toast	French t.	pancakes	Corn Chex	c.muffin	toast
A.M. SNACK (CHOOSE TWO)							
Milk	milk		milk			milk	milk
Fruit, veg or Juice				apple	applesauce		
Bread or alternate	crackers	celery	soft pretzel		cookies	crackers	crackers
Meat or alternate	cheese	yogurt	cheese	hot dog		beef jerky	
LUNCH							
Milk	MILK	MILK	MILK	MILK	MILK	MILK	MILK
Meat or alternate	hot dog	ham	fish	chicken	beef	ham	beef
Fruit or veg	gr. beans	pineapple	potato	gr. salad	tomato	pineapple	corn
Fruit or veg	pickles	carrots	peas	corn	pickles	celery	pickles
Bread or alternate	bun	roll	cornbread	roll	bun	bread	bun
P.M. SNACK (CHOOSE TWO)							
Milk	milk	milk	milk		milk	milk	
Fruit, veg or Juice	grape j.	banana		apple		carrots	apple j.
Bread or alternate	gr. cracker		blueberry muffin	bagel	cookies		crackers
Meat or alternate				tuna			cheese
DINNER							
Milk	MILK	MILK	MILK	MILK	MILK	MILK	MILK
Meat or alternate	chicken	ham	meat sauce	beef	turkey	fish	chicken
Fruit or veg	potato	potato	gr. beans	potato	pears	peas	corn
Fruit or veg	broccoli	gr. salad	applesauce	gr. salad	spinach	peaches	spinach
Bread or alternate	bread	roll	pasta	bread	rice	rice	roll
LATE NIGHT SNACK (CHOOSE TWO)							
Milk		milk	milk			milk	milk
Fruit, veg or Juice	raisins				apple j.		apple
Bread or alternate	crackers	cookies	crackers	bread	crackers	crackers	
Meat or alternate			tuna	egg salad			

NOTIFICATION OF PARENT'S RIGHTS

Parent's Rights

1. Parents/guardians, upon presentation of identification, have the right to enter and inspect the child day care facility, in which their child(ren) are receiving care, without advance notice to the provider. Entry and inspection right is limited to the normal operating hours while their child(ren) is receiving care.
2. The law prohibits discrimination or retaliation against any child or parent/guardian for exercising his/her right to inspect the facility.
3. The law requires this notice of parents/guardians be notified of their rights to enter and inspect.
4. The law requires that this notice of parent's rights to enter and inspect be posted in the facility in a location accessible to parents/guardians.
5. The law authorizes the person in charge of the child day care facility to deny access to a parent/guardian under the following circumstances:
    a) The parent/guardian is behaving in a way which poses a risk to children in the facility, or
    b) The adult is a noncustodial parent and the facility has been requested in writing by the custodial parent to not permit access to the noncustodial parent.

(Detach Here)

ACKNOWLEDGMENT OF
PARENT'S RIGHTS NOTIFICATION

This will acknowledge that I/we, the parents of _____, have received a copy of "PARENT'S RIGHTS" from the licensee or authorized representative of _____.

(Name of Facility)

_____   _____
Signature of Parent(s)/Guardian(s)   Date

NOTE: Bottom portion of this form shall be retained in the child's file.

Weekly Attendance Sheet

MONTH:				WEEK:				YEAR:			
CHILD'S NAME:		**CHILD'S NAME:**		**CHILD'S NAME:**		**CHILD'S NAME:**		**CHILD'S NAME:**		**CHILD'S NAME:**	
MONDAY		MONDAY		MONDAY		MONDAY		MONDAY		MONDAY	
IN	OUT	IN	OUT	IN	OUT	IN	OUT	IN	OUT	IN	OUT
CHARGES:		*CHARGES:*		*CHARGES:*		*CHARGES:*		*CHARGES:*		*CHARGES:*	
TUESDAY		TUESDAY		TUESDAY		TUESDAY		TUESDAY		TUESDAY	
IN	OUT	IN	OUT	IN	OUT	IN	OUT	IN	OUT	IN	OUT
CHARGES:		*CHARGES:*		*CHARGES:*		*CHARGES:*		*CHARGES:*		*CHARGES:*	
WEDNESDAY		WEDNESDAY		WEDNESDAY		WEDNESDAY		WEDNESDAY		WEDNESDAY	
IN	OUT	IN	OUT	IN	OUT	IN	OUT	IN	OUT	IN	OUT
CHARGES:		*CHARGES:*		*CHARGES:*		*CHARGES:*		*CHARGES:*		*CHARGES:*	
THURSDAY		THURSDAY		THURSDAY		THURSDAY		THURSDAY		THURSDAY	
IN	OUT	IN	OUT	IN	OUT	IN	OUT	IN	OUT	IN	OUT
CHARGES:		*CHARGES:*		*CHARGES:*		*CHARGES:*		*CHARGES:*		*CHARGES:*	
FRIDAY		FRIDAY		FRIDAY		FRIDAY		FRIDAY		FRIDAY	
IN	OUT	IN	OUT	IN	OUT	IN	OUT	IN	OUT	IN	OUT
CHARGES:		*CHARGES:*		*CHARGES:*		*CHARGES:*		*CHARGES:*		*CHARGES:*	
TOTAL CHARGES:		**TOTAL CHARGES:**		**TOTAL CHARGES:**		**TOTAL CHARGES:**		**TOTAL CHARGES:**		**TOTAL CHARGES:**	

CHILD DAY-CARE ROSTER

FACILITY NAME		FACILITY LICENSE NUMBER:		DATE/UPDATE:		
CHILD'S NAME/ BIRTHDATE	ADDRESS	PARENT/GUARDIAN NAME(S)	DAYTIME PHONE OF PARENT/GUARDIAN	PHYSICIAN NAME AND PHONE	DATE ENROLLED	DATE LEFT

AUTHORIZATION OF MEDICATION

Name of child: _____

Name and prescription number of the medication to be given: _____
_____

Specific instructions for administering medication:

    Dosage - _____

    Method of administration - _____
    _____
    _____
    _____

    Dates and time of day medication is to be given - _____
    _____

    Reason the medication is given - _____
    _____
    _____
    _____

Signature of parent or guardian: _____

Date of authorization: _____

RECORD OF MEDICATION

Name of child: _____

Name and prescription number of medication: _____

_____

Date: _____   Time: _____   Dosage: _____

Date: _____   Time: _____   Dosage: _____

Date: _____   Time: _____   Dosage: _____

Date: _____   Time: _____   Dosage: _____

Date: _____   Time: _____   Dosage: _____

Date: _____   Time: _____   Dosage: _____

Date: _____   Time: _____   Dosage: _____

Method by which medication was administered: _____

_____

_____

_____

Signature: _____

SUSPECTED CHILD-ABUSE REPORTING FORM

The following information was provided to:

_____

(*Name of Person/Agency*)

_____

(*Telephone Number/Address*)

Child's Name : _____   Date of Birth: _____

Address: _____

_____

Parents' Names: _____

Address: _____

_____

Phone Number: _____

PHYSICAL INDICATORS OBSERVED:

_____

_____

_____

_____

BEHAVIORAL INDICATORS OBSERVED:

_____

_____

_____

_____

OTHER INDICATOR'S OBSERVED/KNOWN:

_____

_____

_____

_____

Reporter's Name and Position: _____

Signature: _____

Date of Report: _____

TRANSPORTATION PERMISSION

_____ is authorized to transport
Child Care Provider's Name

_____ for field trips and other activities
Child's Name

which are supervised by the provider.

EACH CHILD MUST HAVE WRITTEN PERMISSION FOR THE CHILD CARE PROVIDER
TO FURNISH TRANSPORTATION

SIGNATURE OF PARENT OR LEGAL GUARDIAN	DATE

LOG OF ACCIDENTS, INJURIES OR ILLNESSES

DATE	TIME	CHILD'S NAME	PROBLEM AND LOCATION OF ACCIDENT	TYPE OF TREATMENT PROVIDED	WITNESSES	WHEN PARENT(S) OR GUARDIAN(S) WERE NOTIFIED

DAY CARE CLOSET

SMALL TOYS

LARGE TOYS

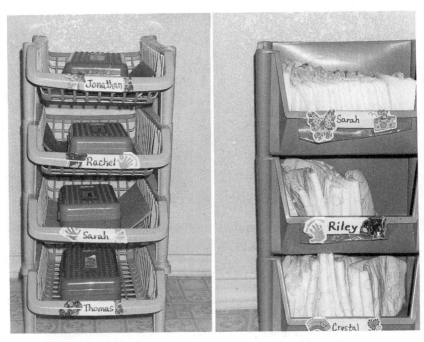

CHILDREN'S BASKETS   **DIAPERS**

VALENTINE'S CAKES

Appendix B

Note: In order to use the materials provided in this section, flannelboard figures and crafts should be enlarged to a size of 8½″ x 11″.

ZOO ANIMALS

Items needed: two paper plates, stapler, hole punch, string or yarn, pictures of animals, contact paper (if desired), crayons or washable markers.

Cut one paper plate in half. Let children staple edges together to make a pocket. Have children color a zoo animal and glue on the front. Write the words "Zoo Animals" at the top. Punch a hole at the top/center and tie a string through. (These can be hung up, taken home later and hung on the child's door.)

Have children color the zoo animal pictures following and cover them with clear contact paper, if desired. Put in the pocket.

ZOO ANIMALS (cont.)

ALLIGATOR

Example:

Pattern: Cut out pattern and tape or glue alligator together. Use green construction paper and cut out alligator and top head piece using pattern. Have children attach the head by matching the X's and securing with a brad. Mouth will open and shut. Have children glue white ric-rac on lines of mouth for teeth.

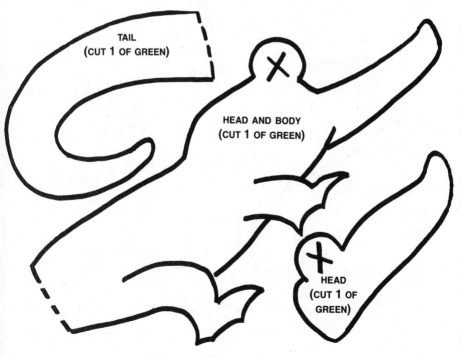

A TOUCHING BOOK

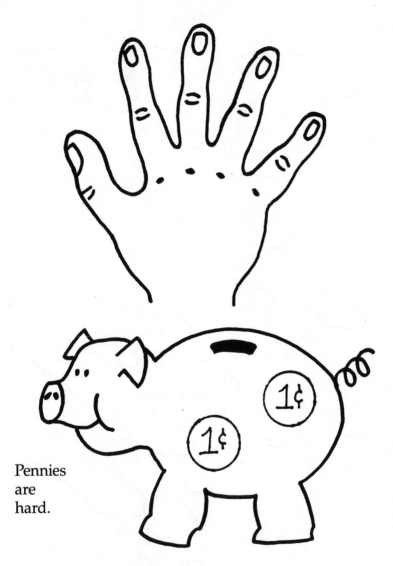

Pennies
are
hard.

(GLUE PENNIES IN THE PIGGY BANK.)

A TOUCHING BOOK (cont.)

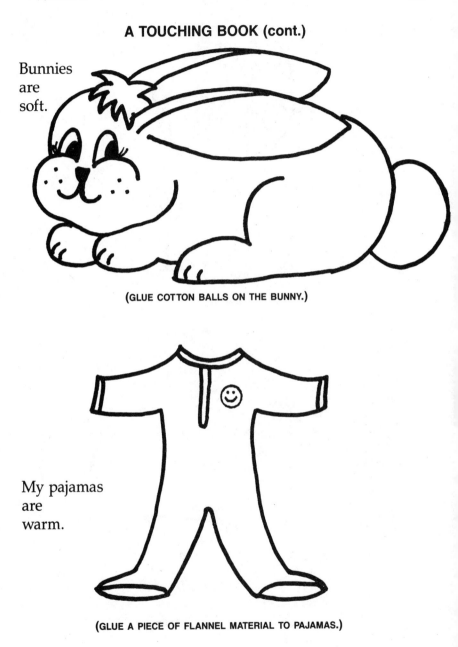

Bunnies
are
soft.

(GLUE COTTON BALLS ON THE BUNNY.)

My pajamas
are
warm.

(GLUE A PIECE OF FLANNEL MATERIAL TO PAJAMAS.)

Bubble gum
is
sticky.

(COLOR THE GUMBALLS.)

The sand in my
sandbox is
scratchy.

(GLUE SANDPAPER IN THE SANDBOX.)

A crocodile's
teeth are
sharp.

(GLUE POPCORN KERNELS IN MOUTH.)

My kitten
is
soft.

(GLUE A PIECE OF FAKE FUR TO KITTEN.)

SONG "FIVE LITTLE SPECKLED FROGS"
FLANNELBOARD FIGURES

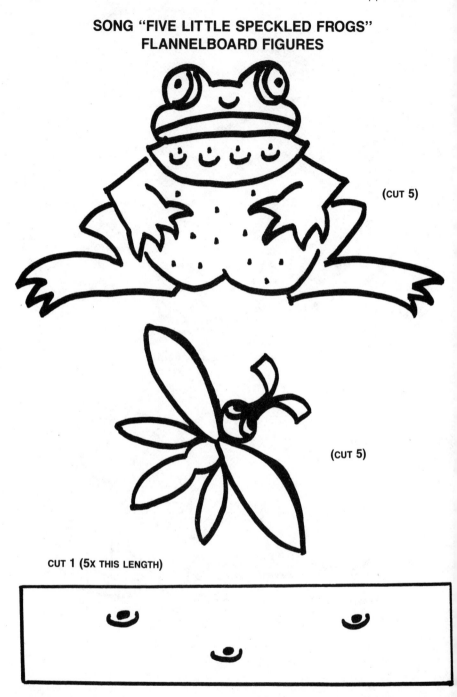

(CUT 5)

(CUT 5)

CUT 1 (5X THIS LENGTH)

SONG "FIVE LITTLE SPECKLED FROGS"
FLANNELBOARD FIGURES (cont.)

THE LITTLE RED HEN
FLANNELBOARD FIGURES

RED HEN

(CUT 1 OF RED OR ORANGE)

RED HEN (cont.)

Directions: Use a brown paper lunch sack for the body. Have children stuff with newspaper so it will stand up. Tape top closed. Have children glue feet on bottom of sack—folded so they stick out. Have them glue eyes and beak to upper body. Then glue paper body to sack. Have them glue red or orange feathers in the back.

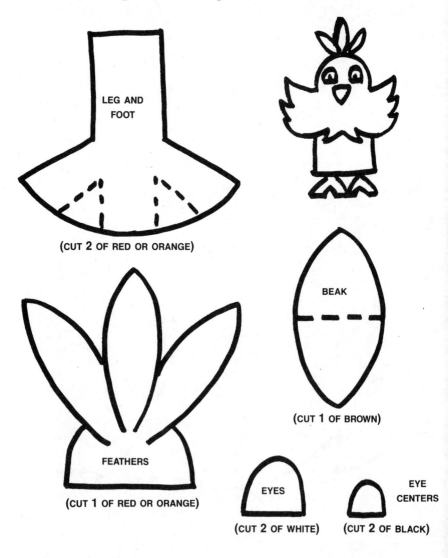

LEG AND
FOOT

(CUT 2 OF RED OR ORANGE)

FEATHERS

(CUT 1 OF RED OR ORANGE)

BEAK

(CUT 1 OF BROWN)

EYES

(CUT 2 OF WHITE)

EYE
CENTERS

(CUT 2 OF BLACK)

CINDERELLA
FLANNELBOARD FIGURES

CINDERELLA FLANNELBOARD FIGURES (cont.)

LITTLE RED RIDING HOOD
FLANNELBOARD FIGURES

THE SHEPHERD BOY AND THE WOLF
FLANNELBOARD FIGURES

THE TORTOISE AND THE HARE
FLANNELBOARD FIGURES

VALENTINE RABBIT

Directions: Cut out pattern pieces on page 167 from construction paper. Have children glue the pieces to an 8½" x 11" sheet of white construction paper to form rabbit, as shown. Draw on the eyes and tail. Use white curling ribbon for the whiskers.

VALENTINE RABBIT (cont.)

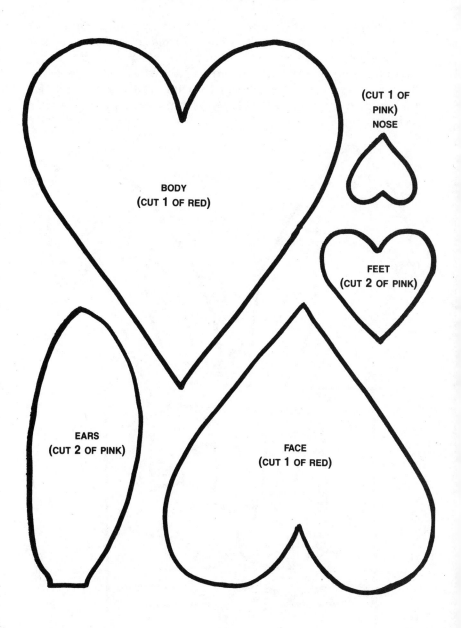

RABBIT SACK

Directions: While lunch bag is still folded up, lay this pattern on top and cut out. Cut out two eyes and bow tie from colored construction paper and have children glue on. Glue a pink pom-pom on for a nose. Draw on eyebrows. Make whiskers from black construction paper for children to glue on. Make pink ears with white centers and let children glue on. Make a handle out of construction paper, double thickness, and staple on.

WITCH PUPPET

Directions: Cut one chin from light green construction paper. Have children glue chin under flap on a brown paper lunch sack. Cut one light green face. Have children glue to bottom of lunch sack (flap) before gluing hat on. Have children glue black or green curling ribbon (curled by running along a scissor blade) on sides of face for hair. Have children glue black hat on top of head. Let children draw on scary eyes, nose, and mouth to face.

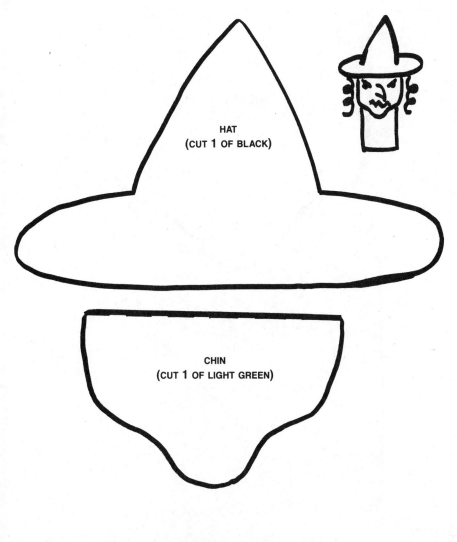

HAT
(CUT 1 OF BLACK)

CHIN
(CUT 1 OF LIGHT GREEN)

WITCH PUPPET (cont.)

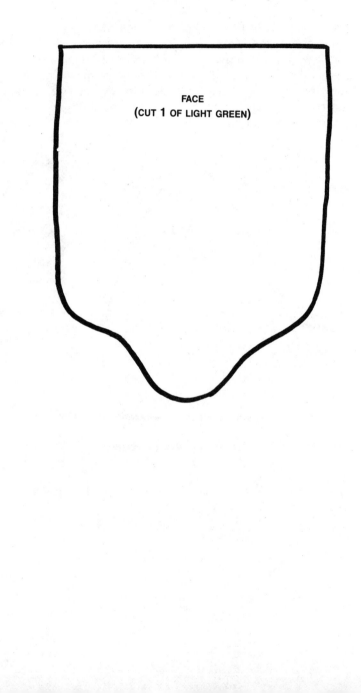

FACE
(CUT 1 OF LIGHT GREEN)

BLACK SPIDER

Directions: Use eight 8″ x 1″ strips of black construction paper for legs. Stack on top of each other and poke a brad through the top. Secure and spread legs out. Have children glue yellow eyes to two legs. Let children curl the legs by rolling on a pencil. Tie a piece of yarn around the top and hang from the ceiling or ceiling fan.

DANCING JACK-O'-LANTERN

Directions: Cut out a pumpkin from a large piece of orange construction paper. Have children draw on a face with black marker and fill in. Have children glue on a stem cut from green construction paper. For hair, add some green curling ribbon, curled. For arms, use 12″ x 2″ strips of black construction paper. For legs, use 18″ x 2″ black strips. Have children fold back and forth accordion style. Trace child's hand and feet onto yellow paper. Cut out and glue or staple to arms and legs. Glue or staple arms and legs to pumpkin, as shown in sketch.

BOUNCY TAIL BLACK CAT

Directions: Cut out head, eyes, ears, nose, and whiskers. Have
children glue on to face. Draw a line from nose to mouth. Draw on
mouth. Let children glue head to body. Have children glue tail to
body, as shown in sketch.

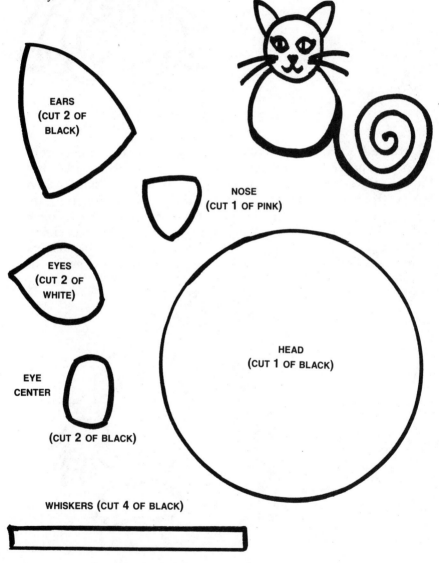

EARS
(CUT 2 OF
BLACK)

NOSE
(CUT 1 OF PINK)

EYES
(CUT 2 OF
WHITE)

HEAD
(CUT 1 OF BLACK)

EYE
CENTER

(CUT 2 OF BLACK)

WHISKERS (CUT 4 OF BLACK)

BOUNCY TAIL BLACK CAT (cont.)

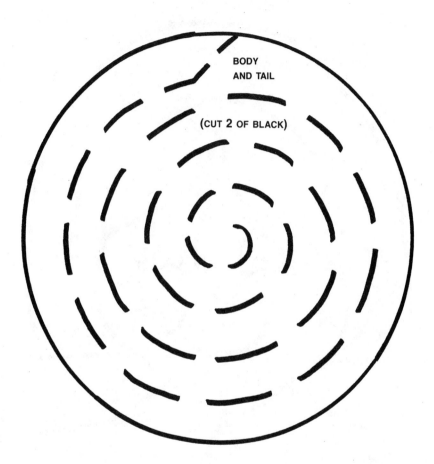

Cut two of these circles out of black construction paper. Leave one solid for body. Cut the other one on the dotted line to make a long bouncy tail. This cat can be hung up with yarn for all to see.

PILGRIM GIRL

PILGRIM BOY

MR. CURLY TAIL TURKEY

Directions: Cut out turkey from brown construction paper. Cut ten of
the feather pattern from various colors. Color a face on the turkey.
Curl each colored band around a pencil and glue to the turkey's back
for feathers.

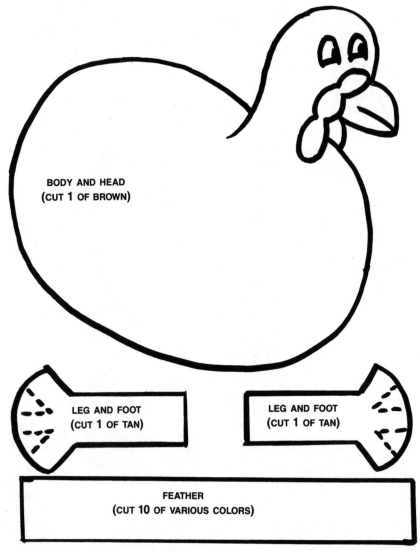

BODY AND HEAD
(CUT 1 OF BROWN)

LEG AND FOOT
(CUT 1 OF TAN)

LEG AND FOOT
(CUT 1 OF TAN)

FEATHER
(CUT 10 OF VARIOUS COLORS)

RED-NOSED REINDEER SURPRISE BAG

Directions: Put a surprise in a brown lunch sack for each child. Then fold "A" in on dotted line. Fold "B" down on dotted line, as shown in sketch. Glue or staple the antlers in place. Glue two eyes on. Close sack shut by gluing on the red nose.

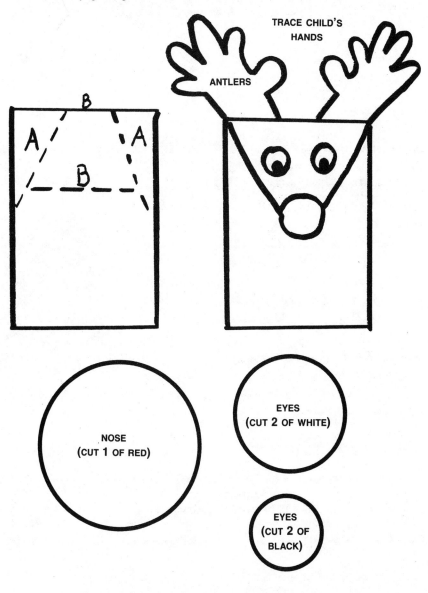

Dear Parents,

I am planning to have a Santa's Secret Shop at Carolyn's
Child Care on December 11. This will
be like playing store, but the children
get to buy gifts (inexpensive items I
will have purchased) that they can
give to family members as surprises
from them. If you would like to
participate, please put the number of
gifts you would like the child to buy in
the boxes, so I will have an idea of
how many to buy. To keep this fun
and affordable the cost of the gifts will
be $1.00 each. If you want 2 gifts, the
child should bring $2.00. We will also have fun wrapping
our own gifts that day.

Please put a number in the box to indicate how many
gifts:

❑ Daddy   ❑ Mommy   ❑ Grandpa   ❑ Grandma

❑ Sister   ❑ Brother   ❑ Other